MW00387544

THE FAMILY
IDEA
BOOK
TWO

THE FAMILY IDEA BOOK TWO

Mina S. Coletti
and
Roberta Kling Giesea

Deseret Book Company
Salt Lake City, Utah

Printed in the United States of America

First printing October 1982
Second printing July 1985

Library of Congress Cataloging in Publication Data

Coletti, Mina S., 1945–
The family idea book II.

Includes index.
1. Family—Religious life—Miscellanea.
2. Child rearing—Miscellanea. 3. Mormon Church—Doctrinal and controversial works—Miscellanea.
I. Giesea, Roberta Kling, 1944– II. Title.
BX8643.F3C64 1982 649′.7 82-14612
ISBN 0-87747-925-9 (pbk.)

To our husbands and our eleven children, with love:
Ed, Dori, Todd, Kristin, Elizabeth, John, and Kathleen Coletti
John, John Jr., Heather, Spencer, Jeffrey, and Todd Giesea

CONTENTS

PREFACE

In 1980 Deseret Book published our first volume, *The Family Idea Book*. Many readers of that book shared with us ideas that have worked in their families.

In this volume, we have taken the creative beginnings of *The Family Idea Book* a few steps further in the areas of Sabbath day, family home evening, traditions, and organization. We are doubly excited by the opportunity to add new sections on such topics as culture in the home, fathers, building character in children, and beating the blahs.

We are confident that, as readers sample ideas that are specifically relevant to them, they will grow, feel freer, and be more successful. We know because this has been our very special experience as we have read, learned from you, and prepared to share these accumulated suggestions with you and your family.

We give this work to you with a feeling of love in our hearts and a prayer that you will know hope and success in your life.

ACKNOWLEDGMENTS

We wish to express our gratitude to those who have graciously shared their ideas with us:

Mary Ann Marshall, Diane Pace, Elizabeth Bates, Maude Fairbanks, Dana Thelin, Donna Lowe, Michelle Broadbent, Connie Kling, Leona Grover, Dixie Jaques, Sally Adams, Fae Bromley, Janet and Hank Schultz, Beth Clawson, Sonja Jensen, Lois Fontana, June Koyle, Mary Grace Allen, Venette Weeks, Tami Berry, Cheri Owen, Judith Beverly, John and Sandy Keating.

Dr. Gary Bunnell, Anne Tobin, Bertha Riggs, Renee Willits, Sue Kjar, Patricia Steiner, Paula Elliott, Carol Francis, Sue George, Darlyn Calvi, Jeanie and Dina Mastrandrea, Stacey Yates, Mele Leger, Chris May, Peggy Roberts, Jean Goff, Linda Pearson, Judy Llewellen, Butch Bush, Fred and Ann Groven, Janis Rippon, Christina Clark.

Rhea Hornbeck, Winnie May, Carol Bradshaw, Judy Dale, Jill Culbertson, Dixie Vogel, Val Gividen, Peggy Anderson, Sherry Bookman, De Ann Nielsen, Kathy Fengel, Betty Dufur, Pam Greenan, Marianne Harris, Linda Stout, Debbie Bean, Alice Bolen, Dorothy Gruenwald, the Quinteros, Kathleen Baer, Adele Coray, Vangie Allen Blau, Jean Funk, Ruth Talbot, Beth Gotfredson, Joan Thomsen, Suzanne Limburg, Evelyn Stout, Sandy Hollingsworth, Dr. Michael Draper, Kay Williams, and Lynette Thomsen.

Special thanks to Marcia Santolucita and Wendy Giacomini for their reliability and efficiency in typing the manuscript.

1

BUILDING CHARACTER IN CHILDREN

Train up a child
in the way he should go:
and when he is old,
he will not depart
from it.
(Proverbs 22:6)

"TRAIN UP A CHILD"

Life Is a School

A child's world is like a school, where he is being taught each day to become an adult. The kind of adult he will be is determined by the self-concepts he develops as a child. When my children make mistakes, I tell them, "It's all right to make mistakes. It's how you handle them that matters." I remind them that they don't know all that I know about life. How can they, when I'm thirty and they're under ten? They are here to learn those things I already know; I am here to guide. This makes sense to them, and they will then listen if I speak softly and patiently, without irritation.

What Is Maturity?

We try to teach our children that they are growing to maturity. We tell them that a mature person has:

1. Understanding of who he is—his strengths and weaknesses.
2. Self-respect and self-acceptance.
3. Concern and respect for others.
4. Self-control.
5. Ability to make wise decisions.
6. Ability to assume responsibility for his own motives, decisions, and actions
7. Positive character traits.

Caught, Not Taught

I realize that character is caught rather than taught. This puts a great responsibility for a child's character squarely upon the shoulders of his parents, because it is what we *do* rather than what we *say* that will affect him. My goals are to:

—never speak negatively about others.

—speak gently and kindly. Sometimes a whisper will get more attention than a yell.

—laugh with the children; see the funny side of life.

—listen to each child, seeing beyond his words.

—never compare a child to his brothers and sisters.

—never laugh at a child or his questions.

A Learning Experience

All of life's experiences are potential forces for learning, for building character. I teach my children to ask, "What can I learn from that experience?" Sometimes the answer is merely "to grow strong" or "to handle disappointment without crying."

Perspective

I try to keep in mind that one day I will have to let this child go, so at each stage of development I let go of him in areas where he shows independence. I do not want him to be dependent on me emotionally or physically when he reaches adulthood. If the letting go has been a gradual process, as it should be, we have no problems.

IDEAS FOR REINFORCEMENT

Awards
We occasionally give blue ribbons or certificates of achievement to promote good character traits in our children. Praising them really works! The following is an example of an award:

For outstanding achievement in

____,
(Character Trait)

we hereby present this award to

____,
(Name)

SIGNED,

____
(Parent's name)

____
(Parent's name)

You Take the Cake
We present a "You Take the Cake" award to a child who shows remarkable improvement in a character trait. The cake is presented with words of praise during family home evening. The person may choose to share the cake with others or to eat the entire cake himself.

Heroes and Heroines
We asked each of our children to think of a person he or she admired. They were then to list adjectives describing their heroes' character traits. We asked each to read his list and give examples of incidents that demonstrated these traits. Later, we compiled the information on each list and gave it to the admired individual.

I'm Like a . . .
Self-knowledge is very important to growth. We encourage our children to create similes, comparing themselves to objects:

"I'm like a pencil. I go dull without being sharpened with correction."

"I'm like a bottle of ketchup. Squeeze me and I spurt out lots of love."

"I'm like Scotch tape. I'll stick to you through thick and thin."

Give a Talk
When one of my children has a particular problem with a character trait, I will ask his Sunday School teacher to assign him to talk on that particular trait. He will then have to do research on it and will be aware of it in his own development.

Visual Growth

To encourage growth in a particular character trait, we created visual aids to hang on the family bulletin board as an illustration and reminder of the desired growth. Examples:

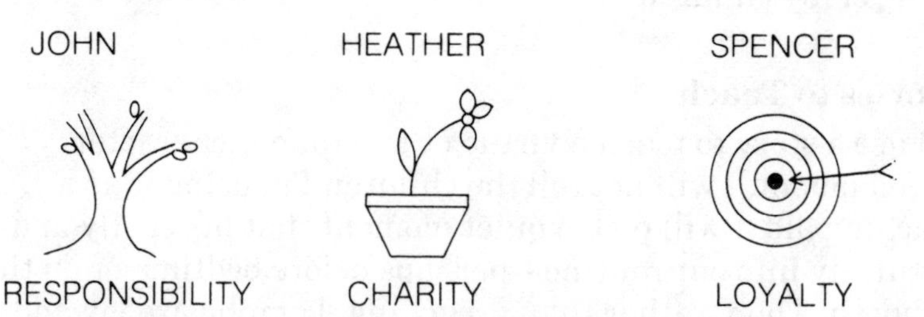

Each time an act is performed exhibiting the trait, a leaf, petal, or arrow is added.

Motto for the Week

We select one value and ask each person to collect as many sayings or mottoes as he can find relating to it. We read and share these thoughts during family home evening, discussing the meaning of each. Finally, we select one as a motto for the following week.

Zion's Child

To encourage our children to live righteously, we have set up a "Zion's Child" bulletin board. When a child exhibits a desirable character trait, his name goes up on the board, along with a brief explanation of what he did:

SELF-RELIANCE

"Spencer dumped the garbage without reminders for three days in a row."

CHARITY

"Todd shared his scooter with Jeffrey."

HONESTY

"Jeffrey admitted he ate all the cookies."

Make-Believe Reinforcement

Sometimes I'll tell stories about make-believe characters, such as "Sloppy Steven" or "Interrupting Isabelle," who get themselves into trouble because of character traits similar to those of my children.

Stories to Teach

If I use a story to teach a virtue or to enhance character development, I will not tell the children I'm using it as a teaching aid. I will pick a quiet moment that fits easily and naturally into our routine—perhaps before bedtime or on the Sabbath. Then, rather than preaching, I emphasize joy and humor.

Quotation Book

Our children have started to compile their own individual quotation books. One daughter draws pictures next to each entry, while another child records his feelings about the quotation. The children collect quotations from talks, articles, or statements they hear. Some are humorous, while others are quite serious. It's interesting to see how the selected thoughts reflect the personality of the collector.

Banner for Quality

I asked my children to each adopt one character trait to work on for the entire year, such as honesty, courage, or faith. Each then cut out or drew symbols for a banner (made of Pellon or felt) to represent his chosen trait. These banners hang on their bedroom doors for a year. At the end of the year, each child will choose a new quality and make a new banner. The child must know the meaning of the trait he chooses, and be able to cite examples of how he lives it.

SYMBOLS:
DIGNITY
STRENGTH
STABILITY

SERENITY
CALM
QUIET

GLORY
INTELLIGENCE

BEAUTY
CHARM
GRACE

Collection of Goods

We gave each of our children a shoe box to decorate as he or she wished. We suggested they cut a slit in the lid and then cover the box with contact paper. They were then told to select a character trait they wanted to develop. They were to collect and place in their boxes sayings, stories, magazine articles, or pictures they found during the month that reminded them of the trait. At the end of the month, we shared the treasures. My daughter included a rose petal in her box because it reminded her of charity. She said the rose gave beauty to all even though, in order to do so, it would die in the vase.

Self-Analysis

We use the following questions to help our children evaluate their own characters:

Courage

1. Are you at ease before strangers or superiors?
2. Do you follow your own convictions?
3. Do you meet your problems courageously without attempting to evade them?

Self-confidence

1. Are you sure of yourself at all times?
2. Do you start things with confidence rather than doubt?
3. Do you back your own judgments with confidence?

Self-discipline

1. Can you shoulder responsibility without worry?
2. Do you control your temper and words?

3. Do you constantly look for opportunities to better yourself?

4. Are you wholeheartedly interested in your work and assignments?

5. Do you carefully observe your daily work to improve it?

6. Do you avoid giving offense through loss of temper or by sarcastic remarks?

7. Do you avoid saying things for which you later become sorry?

Honesty

1. Are you trustworthy in little things?
2. Do you keep your promises and appointments?
3. Do you never lie or cheat?
4. Is your word as good as your bond?
5. Is your mind focused on high ideals of life and service?

Charity

1. Do you get along well with all people?
2. Do you endeavor to lead rather than to boss people?
3. Do you consider the feelings of others?
4. Are you more interested in giving than in getting?

Values Lesson

The following is an example of a form we give to our children when we want them to focus on an example of a particular value or character trait. They are to read from the Book of Mormon, the Bible, a novel, or the newspaper. They then fill in the form:

____
Name

____
Date

Example of ______________ in ______________
Character Trait — Name of work or story

WHO ______________ WHEN ______________
Name of Character — Time

WHERE ______________ WHY ______________
Setting — Reason

The most valuable lesson I learned from this story is:

____

____

OBEDIENCE TO PARENTS

Guidance versus Punishment

I feel that when children make mistakes, they aren't "being bad," but merely need guidance. They are learning to become mature. Trial and error will teach them many valuable lessons in life. Often an explanation of cause and effect is more constructive than punishment.

Parents Give Respect

My husband and I have certain rules governing ourselves as parents. We feel we should give our children respect, just as we expect it for ourselves, so we:

—don't open their mail.

—extend the courtesy of knocking before entering their rooms.

—don't take their things without asking their permission.

—are courteous when speaking to them.

Natural Consequence

When I find the need to exact a punishment, I try to make it as close to a natural consequence as possible. For instance, our children kept coming into our bedroom during a "quiet" time when they had been instructed to stay in their rooms.

The natural result was that they had to stand with their hands on the doorknob, one at a time, for a set period of time. "Since you enjoy turning the doorknob so much, you get to touch it for five minutes," I told them.

The Answer Is No

When I'm in doubt as to whether or not to give permission for something, I say "no." It's always easier to change a no to a yes than it is to turn a yes into a no. Any begging, however, yields nothing. If I change the no later, it will come only after due consideration.

Shared Responsibility

When my children have trouble behaving, I ask them, "What are you going to do about this?" "How do you plan to correct this situation?" "What do you feel would be the appropriate consequence if you fail?" I have found that if I get the children to write out their own commitments and punishments—and if I am consistent in assessing and reassessing progress—then their solutions are just as effective as mine would be. This process also reduces friction and conflict because they are the ones doing the planning and they can't blame me for harshness or injustice.

Finding the Balance

Sometimes I feel like a stagecoach driver. I have to know when to hold the reins tightly and when to loosen them enough to give the horses sufficient freedom to move. Finding a comfortable balance between freedom and restraint is not easy, but it must be done if parents are to be successful. I find the aid of the Holy Ghost indispensable in raising my children. If I didn't hear his voice telling me, "Don't say anything right now," or "Why don't you find out the reason," I would have made more serious errors than I have already.

It's the Rule!

Inconsistency was a real problem in our home. We have learned firsthand the need to sit down with the children, preassess the situation, and then decide on rules and commitments with which all agree. Everyone signs the agreement. Then, the minute the rules are broken, we reassess, redefine, and recommit. It takes time and attention, but it is the best disciplining method we have found. The children enjoy being part of their own training. Some of our family rules that are *never* to be violated are:

—No entering locked doors.

—No going to bed without giving Mom and Dad good-night kisses.

—No talking to someone who is involved in a phone conversation.

When It Hurts to Discipline . . .

When it's painful for my husband and me to correct our children, we remember the story of the priest Eli, in 1 Samuel, chapters 2-4. The Lord cursed Eli's wicked sons and held Eli responsible for failing to restrain them.

Ask in Private

If my child wants to invite another child to stay overnight, come for dinner, or play at our house, and he asks permission in that child's presence, I always say sweetly, "You know the rule. Whenever you ask me in front of your guest, the answer is *always* no." This instantly prevents a recurrence of an embarrassing situation.

Bedtime Struggles

I seemed to be constantly struggling with my preschoolers at bedtime. They didn't want to settle down to sleep after their bedtime stories and prayers. One night I let them look at books before falling asleep. I found that they shortly put the books down and rolled over to go to sleep with no reminders and no fuss. Now I allow time for "book looking" before sleep.

Just Obey, Don't Question

Sometimes I don't have time to explain why I want to have my child do something, or to listen to his discussion of the topic. At these times, I'll say, "Do what I ask you right now; then when there's time after dinner, I'll listen to your feelings."

Time Limits

I find that the children will respond better to time limits if I give them adequate warnings. I say: "When the hands reach here on the clock, I will expect you to put your toys away," or "I'm setting the timer for five minutes. When it rings, it will be time for . . ."

Correct with Tenderness

When we have problems, I will put my child on my lap or put my arm around him and say: "I love you, but we don't do that," or "You are mine for all eternity."

Simple Games

"Mother, May I?" and "Simon Says" are games that teach obedience. Any games with directions for following a leader provide good practice in being obedient.

Commandment with Blessing

"Did you know that the Lord gives a commandment to you to honor your parents?" I ask my children. I will then ask them what it means to honor someone. When they answer, "To obey," which is part of honoring, I will point out the beautiful blessing attached to keeping that commandment: "Honour thy father and thy mother: that thy days may be long upon the land which the Lord thy God giveth thee." (Exodus 20:12.)

Quick Quips

"'No' is 'no' today, tomorrow, and the next day, so don't ask."

"Your behavior is that of an animal. Which animal are you pretending to be today?"

"You're above that kind of behavior."

"You keep trying to convince me you're that way, but I refuse to believe it."

"What is the rule concerning it?"

"Is that what you really want to do?"

"That's the end of that."

"Tomorrow starts a new day."

"It's all right to make errors. It's how you handle them that matters."

"What could you have done differently?"

"I admire those who admit their faults."

"When your room is clean, you may come in for dinner."

"Do you want to be grounded, or do you want to scrub the floors?"

"Here's the sponge. You'd better clean it up."

OBEDIENCE TO GOD

With Exactness

My children love to hear about the little band of two thousand and sixty young men who fought desperately against the Lamanites in one of the Book of Mormon battles. Not one of the men was killed, because of their faith that there was a just God who would preserve them.

"Yea, and they did obey and observe to perform every word of command with exactness; yea, and even according to their faith it was done unto them; and I did remember the words which they said unto me that their mothers had taught them." (Alma 57:21.) Obedience certainly rewarded them!

I Do His Will

I ask my children, when they complain about having to obey, if they think they are better than Jesus. I then recite this scripture: "I am Jesus Christ; I came by the will of the Father, and I do his will." (D&C 19:24.) Somehow, it eases the pain to know that He has to obey also.

Blessings of Obedience

If my children do not obey me, or have a desire to disobey the commandments of the Lord, I will ask them to look up the following scriptures to see what blessings accompany obedience:

Leviticus 26:4-12—rain, crops, peace, fruitfulness
D&C 59:15-23—fullness of the earth, animals, food
D&C 82:10—"I, the Lord, am bound when ye do what I say."

Don't Disappoint You!

I tell my children, "You made a choice in your premortal existence to come here to this earth, to prove to Heavenly Father and yourself that you would obey his laws. Now you don't want to disappoint Him or yourself, do you?"

Balance of Obedience and Blessings

Do you want to enjoy blessings? Then be obedient, because all blessings come from obeying God's laws. He is very fair. He has said: "There is a law, irrevocably decreed in heaven before the foundations of this world, upon which all blessings are predicated—And when we obtain any blessing from God, it is by obedience to that law upon which it is predicated." (D&C 130:20-21.)

Whither Shall I Go?

Even though Nephi faced everyone's, including his father's, complaints about having no food because his bow was broken and the other bows had lost their spring, he faithfully made a new weapon. Then he approached his father, asking in perfect faith and obedience, "Whither shall I go to obtain food?" (1 Nephi 16:23.) Would you be as obedient if your father grumbled against you?

Helpful Responses

"Listen to the still, small voice. What does it tell you?"
"Are you going to include that in your journal tonight?"
"I wonder what Heavenly Father is thinking right now."
"Are you hanging onto the iron rod right now?"
"What you do reflects what you are."

SELF-DISCIPLINE

School Work
We tell our children that work for them is school, just as Mommy's work is doing her very best in providing a nice home, and just as Daddy works hard and well to give us all the material possessions we have. The children are expected to work diligently and do their best at their work.

Anger Hurts You
When you become angry, you fill your body with adrenalin, and you are not able to think straight or act right. As someone has said, "Anger is a very poor adviser."

Finish the Job
We teach our children that a job is not complete until they see it through to the end. We don't let them quit a job halfway through.

Tantrums Won't Work
When I threw temper tantrums as a child, it was because I wanted my mother to come to me so that I could be understood. Realizing this helps me when my own children

throw tantrums. I take them to their rooms and tell them I will stay with them to discuss the problem if they quiet down, but I will walk out if they continue their tantrum. After I had walked out on one or two occasions, my son believed me enough the next time to say, "All right. I'll stop." He pulled himself together immediately. I couldn't believe his control!

Stay Calm

I've noticed that if I stay calm, I keep in control of the child. However, if I explode or speak irritably, I lose.

I Want My Own Way

When her brothers were teasing her, I asked my daughter if she wanted to know of an effective way to stop them. My niece perked up, saying, "By crying. That's what I do." How revealing! Children throw tantrums to get what they want. They want to control their parents in order to get their own way. If I can remember this principle, then I will *never* allow a child to win by throwing a tantrum. If tantrums continue beyond preschool age, then I carefully examine what I am doing to reward such behavior.

Tantrums

If my child throws a tantrum, I know it is because he's tired, because he gets his way when he does it, because he's frustrated that I haven't explained something thoroughly, or because I've been unreasonable in my demands. I will isolate him until he is calm enough to discuss the situation rationally. Then I tell him that if he feels I've been unfair, it is his responsibility to learn to handle unfairness. I'm not perfect, and in his life he will encounter many frustrating situations. Crying will not help; stating feelings calmly may.

Adult Tantrums

When an adult shows little self-control and throws tantrums, it is because his parents failed to show him that he has the power within himself to prevent them. Many people say, "I have a bad temper," as though it were something outside themselves that they can't remove. If our children can see that they are the creators of their emotions and are responsible for their actions, they will not lack self-control as adults. Whenever the opportunity arises, I tell them that they are *choosing* to be angry, or that they have the power to change an emotion. I may ask, "Who is in control of you?"

Helpful Sayings

"'I'll try' are the first words to success." "Anger is a wind that blows out the lamp of the mind." "Doing things by halves is worthless, because it may be the other half that counts." "What lies behind us and what lies before us are tiny matters compared to what lies within us." (William Morrow.)

COURAGE

Time for Courage

"What would you do if someone pointed a gun at your head and asked you if you were a Mormon?" I asked our children this question, which started a lively discussion.

We ended the discussion with an example from the life of President Joseph F. Smith, who was accosted by a band of ruffians while returning home from a mission to Hawaii. The leader of the group swore he would kill anyone who was a Mormon. Pointing his gun at Joseph, he demanded, "Are you a 'Mormon'? Fully expecting the gun to discharge Joseph nonetheless answered, "Yes, siree; dyed in the wool; true blue, through and through." The answer, given boldly and without hesitation, completely disarmed the belligerent man, and in bewilderment, all he could do was shake the young missionary's hand and praise him for his courage. The men then rode off and did not molest Joseph and his party further. (Joseph Fielding Smith, comp., *Life of Joseph F. Smith,* Deseret News Press, p. 189.)

I Think I Can

The "Little Engine That Could" said, "I think I can, I think I can." When my daughter felt reluctant to get into the water to learn to swim, I reminded her to say what the "Little Engine That Could" said. She said it and was able to get into the water.

Animalistic Sport

At one time, I was afraid to allow my son the opportunity to wrestle, thinking it was an "animalistic" sport. However, after reading Genesis 32:24-32, I realized that Jacob wrestled and came out a winner, through determination and persistence. His match may have been only spiritual, but he didn't quit. He became strong. I decided that when my son faces spiritual opposition, his experience in wrestling may prepare him with enough self-confidence and initiative to be victorious.

Afraid of the Dark

When my preschooler was afraid of the dark, he would awaken everyone in the house with his crying. We decided we would cure him of his fear by installing a dimmer on his light switch. Each night we would lower it a little more than the night before. With the light diminishing gradually, he was able to overcome his fear of the dark.

Armor of God

I tell my children the Lord wants them to be strong. My job is to prepare them to withstand temptations and the designs evil men will have upon their goodness and strength.

"Wherefore take unto you the whole armour of God, that ye may be able to withstand in the evil day, and having done all, to stand." (Ephesians 6:13.)

No Whining or Crying

When my toddler falls down, she doesn't cry or whine, because she knows I will not run to rescue her. I may redirect her attention by saying something like, "Oh, Shallys, you made a hole in the floor!"

Respect, Not Fear

Oftentimes fear comes to a child because his parents are fearful. For example, if a parent continually says, "Don't go near the deep end of a pool," instead of saying, "Walk slowly around the deep edge of a pool," the child develops an unreasonable fear instead of a healthy respect.

Wasn't That Fun?

When my six-month-old child fell into a pool, I did not panic. I said, "Oh, wasn't that fun? Want to go in again?" and she went for a dip with me immediately. She was unaware of the pending danger, and now she will learn to swim with a healthy attitude.

Quick Quips

"A turtle doesn't make any progress unless it sticks its neck out."

"A grapefruit is a lemon who had his chance and took it."

"It takes strength and courage to apologize."

SELF-CONFIDENCE

They're Ready
Sometimes parents hold their children back from doing things the children are perfectly capable of doing. My son was asking to use a knife to cut his meat long before I thought he was old enough. Yet when I finally allowed him to use it, he managed just fine. Now I make it a policy that, if a child asks, he is ready to at least try.

I try to point out to my child what the consequences of certain actions will be so that he will learn to think ahead. With each thing he learns to do for himself, he will become a more self-reliant individual.

Do It for Yourself
If my child tells me he is doing something because he will get praise from others, I will ask, "Oh, are they in control of you? Aren't you doing it for your own sense of accomplishment? Isn't that more important to you?" The only one I want him to compete with is himself, because if he constantly seeks for outside security, then he will build no inward strength.

Experience Is the Best Teacher
One of my most painful parental tasks has been to let my children learn by trial and error. I have the urge to cushion

them with explanations, but there are times when silence is more effective. For example, when my daughter is making a cake and resents my explanation of the recipe, I have to back off and let her find out "why" for herself.

He Can Do It

If a child asks me to do something he can do for himself, I don't always jump in to do it for him. I may suggest ways he can do it himself. Step-by-step explanations may be helpful, but if I stand back and let him use his own thinking power to solve his problem, I am helping him to develop confidence in his own abilities. He will sense that I know he can do it, and usually he can. He gains confirmation that he can do it as he succeeds.

Praise

Feelings of success can come from praise, if it is administered genuinely. Criticism causes insecurity and self-conscious nervousness. If my daughter receives a "D" on her report card one time and a "C" the next, I will not ask her why she didn't get a "B." Rather, I will tell her that I see progress and that I know she put forth more effort this time. She's learning precept upon precept and is progressing. That is success!

Humility

In order to prevent my child from becoming arrogant, I will praise what he does, trying *not* to give him the sense that he is better than others. "You shared your toy with your brother; isn't that a kind thing to do?"

No, No!

A child is subconsciously trying to determine who he is. Unfortunately, he tends to believe everything he is told. Therefore, we have a few rules for our family members, including Mom and Dad. We *never* tell the child:

—that *he* is bad. What he does may be bad, but not *him*.

—that we won't love him if he does that. Our love far exceeds his behavior.

—that we don't care what he does.

Encourage Interests

Self-confidence comes when a child feels successful. We try to allow each of our children to pursue his interests. Some of the following have helped:

1. Guide him to choose a hobby. Collections of his choice can be encouraged. The Scouting program offers a variety of choices.
2. Get him involved in physical activities. Local sports programs are very beneficial.
3. Spend time with him doing what he wants to do, the way he wants to do it.
4. Support him through a project until it is finished. Encourage him not to quit.

Be a Leader

Leadership experiences are great builders of self-confidence. If you step in to lead, people will usually follow. I teach my children stock phrases, such as, "Come on everyone, let's . . . ," "I think that we shouldn't . . . ," and "I've found that if we do that, this will happen." Sometimes they have to pretend to have confidence, but it works!

I Am Special

I try to teach my children to love themselves. I remind them daily that no one is more valuable or special than they. If they don't understand themselves and have self-assurance, they cannot help others or operate as free spirits.

No Labels

My son seemed to be accident prone. Every time someone spilled a glass of milk or crashed into something, we knew who it was. Pretty soon, he began to say, "I can't do that. I'm too dumb (or clumsy)." I realized he needed some success experiences. I gave him a drinking glass narrow enough for him to wrap his hand around, and allowed no one, including myself to comment when accidents occurred. I handed him a sponge to clean spills up himself, if necessary, but offered no further help. When the pressure eased, he relaxed and outgrew his clumsiness.

Cruel

"Mama, Jeremy said I have big ears and then he started hitting me," cried my little girl one day. I replied, "Honey, you feel that you have big ears now, don't you. Let's look in the mirror to see. Look, they're not even as big as mine. Do your eyes tell you that Jeremy is correct? He was just being cruel. If you believe him, you will be shrinking down to a cruel level."

Helpful Sayings

"The only limitations you have are those you place upon yourself."

"Those who continually talk about themselves are those who have self-doubt."

"Trust your own judgment."

"Never say, 'I can't do that.' Instead, say, 'I have not yet acquired that talent.'"

"Try to do it yourself. If I do it for you, you will not be self-reliant."

"When you're thirty years old, will I be here to ask?"

"Would you like freedom? It comes when you rely on yourself."

"If you can't rely on yourself, on whom can you rely?"

"You have to live with yourself forever."

"You are responsible for your own actions."

"Always give more than you're asked."

"If you know the truth about yourself, no one can harm you."

"Your destiny is to be a god."

"There's no one who can fill your shoes."

"Never run from responsibility. It is your friend who will strengthen you."

HONESTY

Trust Is a Gift
My children believe I can see dishonesty in their eyes if they try to lie to me. Guilt is very obvious in the face of a child, so I've been able to read my children accurately enough that they know they'll get caught if they lie. I tell them that my trust in them is one of the most precious gifts I can give them. If they destroy it by lying, they rob themselves of that gift.

Understand Motive for Lies
I have found that children will lie for many different reasons. One is to get their own way; another is to avoid getting punished. Still another is to appear to be better than others: "I have two television sets in my room." If we can help our children to see why they lie, then we can help them avoid doing it.

Lying Causes Disappointment
When my seven-year-old child had lied repeatedly and I was at my wit's end as to how to help him, I decided to tell him that next Saturday I would be taking him to a nearby amusement park. When Saturday came, he was all excited about going. I then explained to him that I was sorry, but I

had lied to him. We weren't really going. I took the time to discuss with him the disappointment and lack of faith that lying produces. We ended our talk with a prayer and a new commitment from him. It worked!

Weakest Link

I showed my children a paper chain. One of the links was not fastened securely, so when we pulled on it the entire chain fell. I told them that, like the chain, we are only as strong as our weakest characteristic. I reminded them of Samson, whose entire life was ruined because he couldn't keep a secret from Delilah. If we are dishonest in tiny things, then we are dishonest. We can't be partially dishonest.

I Thought I Taught Him

My fourteen-year-old son was caught shoplifting in a department store with several of his friends. I just couldn't believe he would indulge in such a practice. I thought we had taught him from the time he was a tiny baby the value of honoring other people's property. Somehow, being one of the gang superseded his desire for honesty. Did this mean that his self-esteem was so poor that he couldn't stand up for the right? Perhaps. As a result, we took the following measures:

1. We visited the local prison. One inmate we met converted to the Church but couldn't be baptized until he has completed his term. He told us of his frustration and warned my son not to let himself fall into the trap of losing his freedom.

2. We spent more time with my son. I wanted to know what was on his mind and to open the lines of communication, which had started to close.

3. He had to confess to the bishop and fully repent, making restitution.

4. In family home evening, we role-played situations in which one person pretended to influence another to do negative things, while the other would try different methods of avoiding the temptations.

Helpful Sayings

"You can't think crooked and walk straight." (Hugh B. Brown.)

"Dishonesty breeds lack of trust."

"Dare to be true: Nothing can need a lie;/A fault which needs it most, grows two thereby." (Herbert.)

"A good name is rather to be chosen than great riches."

"Clear water pours from pure springs."

"A man that seeks truth and loves it must be reckoned precious to any human society." (Frederick the Great.)

"If you tell the truth, you don't have to remember anything."

"Truth is obeyed when it is loved."

WISE JUDGMENT

Learning Is Sought

"A wise man will hear, and will increase learning; and a man of understanding shall attain unto wise counsels." (Proverbs 1:5.)

I have this proverb framed and hanging in the kitchen. I want my children to know that they must learn from the lessons of life. No experience will be detrimental to them if they can gain some sort of strength from it. They should also consult with those who are wiser than they, such as their earthly or Heavenly Father.

Still, Small Voice

How do I get my children to recognize the still, small voice? The answer is simple: I tell them to listen for it and then obey it. Whenever opportunities arise to call on the Lord, I use them. One day I couldn't find my car keys just as we were about to go to church. I asked everyone to say a prayer and then to just listen for the answer. One of us was prompted to look under the car. That's exactly where the keys were! Another time my daughter was about to set her baby brother on a large rock when she distinctly heard a voice saying, "Heather, don't do that!" If she hadn't listened to the voice, the baby would have fallen off the rock, because it was far too steep.

Which Would You Choose?

We've found that we don't know our children as well as we think we do. To understand them better, we've devised a quiz with questions like the following:

Which is the most effective way to get what you want?

1. Cry—throw a tantrum!
2. Pout and sulk.
3. Say you don't want it anyway.
4. Bribe.
5. Forget about it and think of something else.
6. Beg and beg.

I would be proud of myself if I could:

1. Climb to the top of a mountain.
2. Hold my temper back when brother/sister makes me angry.
3. Help Mom with the cooking.
4. Go to the grocery store for Mom.

Alternatives/Consequences

The following steps help clarify alternatives and consequences whenever a problem needs to be solved:

1. Identify problem.
2. List a variety of solutions.
3. Write negative and positive consequences of each solution.
4. List the action needed for each alternative.
5. Rank the solutions from one to ten—most desirable to least desirable.

Decisions

Certain situations require "walking" the child through the experience beforehand. He will have a better chance of handling himself responsibly if you discuss with him possible ways to resolve the following conflicts:

1. Your end-of-the-year school party is on Sunday. You have been taught to keep the Sabbath holy and your parents say that the decision to attend or not is up to you.
2. You find that your best friend has found a way to sneak into the movie theater without paying. He wants you to join him.
3. You ate all the cookies in the cookie jar. Your parents ask who did it.
4. Your sister told you she smoked a cigarette. Do you tell your parents?
5. You spent all your allowance so you now have no money to spend at the roller-skating party.
6. Your little brother went into your bedroom and messed it up. You think he took some candy you had hidden.
7. Your best friend has invited you to join her family in a trip to an amusement park. However, it is your little sister's birthday, and you had promised your mother you'd help with the birthday party.
8. While Mother was gone, you played football in the living room, a forbidden activity. You hit her favorite vase with the ball and shattered it. You cleaned it up, but do you tell her or not?

Decisions, Decisions, Decisions!

My eleven-year-old son said, "Mom, when I was a little kid, I never knew life was made up of so many decisions to make." I thought about what he said and realized that perhaps I didn't start letting him make decisions at an early age. Yet I always remember giving him choices whenever I could.

"Would you rather wear your blue pants or beige today? Do you want a tuna or bologna sandwich? Would you rather have Daddy or Mommy read to you tonight? What book do you want to hear?" These are examples of decisions he could make at a young age. But I began to think these experiences needed to be enriched.

I devised a game that has no right or wrong answers, but makes the children thoughtfully decide on their responses. My husband and I also participate because it's imaginative and fun. The questioner asks, "Which would you rather be . . ."

—the Book of Mormon or the Doctrine and Covenants?
—a child or a parent?
—Isaac or Abraham?
—Samson or Delilah?
—Lehi or Nephi?
—sun or earth?
—missionary or bishop?
—Liahona or brass plates?
—faith or charity?
—repentance or resurrection?
—string bean or soybean?
—eraser or glue?
—sky or ocean?

Each person has one minute to answer and explain his reason. (Use a timer or stopwatch.) This keeps a fast pace and no one gets bored. No one is ever corrected or ridiculed during the game.

Can't Control Results

An oft-quoted statement at our house is, "You may choose what to do, but you may not choose what the results will be." This is an effective argument when a child says his friends are doing something that I do not approve of.

Helpful Sayings

"Wisdom is not book learning. If you have wisdom, you will obtain knowledge."

"The gift of wisdom is earned."

"He who is wise will think before he acts."

"'I will' is more important than 'I.Q.' "

"Every act, thought, or attitude, every conscious or unconscious decision to do or not to do something either assists in the building or helps in the tearing-down process."

COURTESY

No Teasing

I want my children to understand there is nothing funny about teasing others. Remarks and actions that hurt people do not bring joy. A little reminder, "Are you being kind right now?" usually brings the teaser into focus.

Whispering Is Rude

When my daughter whispered a secret to me in front of her brother, I made her stop to look at him. I told her to ask him what he was feeling. He answered, "I feel like you're talking about me." She wasn't aware until that moment that her action had hurt another.

Are Manners in Order?

We have a decorative framed list of manners within sight of the dinner table:

—Wash hands and face.
—Don't grab—wait your turn.
—Chew with mouth closed.
—Don't lean on elbows.
—Use napkin, and fold it after use.
—Ask to be excused before leaving table.
—Express gratitude to the cook.

Goof-up List

We have a "Goof-up List" hanging on our family bulletin board. Periodically I ask the youngsters to check themselves on each item. Do I:

1. Invite myself over to play at others' homes?
2. Brag? "My daddy's job is more important than yours!"
3. Forget to use manners, such as saying "please," or "thank you?"
4. Talk about someone's funny hairdo, wrinkled dress, or bad manners?
5. Tease someone for being different?
6. Beg to have a bite of someone's cookie, ice cream, or candy?
7. Ask to be first in line or to have the biggest or the best?
8. Constantly whine or complain about others?

More than a Thank-You

In our house, politeness doesn't count unless it radiates genuine thoughtfulness. I teach my children to say, "I enjoyed ______," because it is more specific than a "thank-you."

Accept Compliments Graciously

Accepting compliments graciously with a simple "I'm glad you like it," or "Thank you," is an effective way to avoid radiating arrogance. We teach our children to never apologize if a compliment is extended.

Express Gratitude

If someone in our family fails to send a thank-you note in response to generosity, he may stay in his room until it is completed. There is no excuse for failing to express gratitude.

May I Please?

"Get me . . ." will always be answered in our house by "I'm not your slave." However, if politeness and kindness are expressed—"May I please have . . ."—someone will probably respond positively.

Don't Interrupt

I don't hesitate to tell my children "You're being rude" if they try to interrupt a conversation. They learn quickly that they must wait until others have finished speaking.

Answer When Addressed

If my children do not reply when someone speaks to them, I tell them that they are, without words, expressing to that person that he isn't worth a response. It is very discourteous.

Correct English

If I hear my children using incorrect English, I'll say, "I just heard someone say, 'He got boots.' What do you think he meant?" We discuss the correct usage.

Later we play "Gotcha." Anytime someone makes an error, we say, "Gotcha." No one wants to be caught, so everyone strives to use correct English.

Sloppy Speech

I don't allow my children to answer a question with "Huh?" They can learn at an early age to say, "Pardon me." Also, courtesies such as "Excuse me," and "May I" are always expected.

Don't Be Impertinent

I will tell my children, "Many times you will observe adults failing to play by the rules of life. They may lack courtesy or maturity, but a child should not correct them. People always deserve respect for their age, so give it to them. Never be impertinent."

I Don't Like That

I teach my children that it is very rude to say "I don't like that" while eating. If they don't like something, they are required to at least take a bite. I say, "There will come a time when you will be required to eat something to be polite, so you'd better be familiar with the taste." I encourage them to eat what they don't like first and what they enjoy last. If they refuse the one bite, I say, "Fine. You will eat it all for the next meal."

Respect Belongings of Others

A child should not be allowed to play with another's possessions without permission. Our policy is, "My friend, that belongs to me. Do not touch."

Guests Over to Play

When our children have guests over to play at our house, we say, "You're responsible for your guests. If they don't follow the house rules, you will be held accountable."

CHARITY

A Gift of a Toy

Every once in a while, I clean out the messy toy box. I ask my children to pick out one toy each to give to someone else. I let them decide overnight. The next day, we deliver the "gifts" to the friend's doorstep with a note, "To Elizabeth, from someone who likes you." Or we may ask the recipient's mother to place it under his pillow so he has a surprise that night. Thinking of clever ways to deliver the presents is a joy to us.

Don't Say "I'm Sorry"

When a child has been thoughtless or rude, I never allow him to merely say "I'm sorry." Instead, he must say, "Forgive me for my thoughtlessness (or rudeness)." In this way, he is forced to acknowledge his own error.

Do unto Others

If our children utter any sort of unkind words, we use the "Do unto Others" approach. "Would you like to hear those words uttered about (or to) yourself? How would that make you feel? You keep trying to convince me that you don't care how others feel, but I refuse to believe that of you."

Fasting and Prayer

I invite my children to join me in fasting and praying for others in the ward. We all rejoiced together when we saw the dramatic healing of one sister who was the sole support of her family and who had no insurance to cover expenses of an upcoming operation. After we fasted and prayed, she found the operation was not necessary, and she was able to continue working.

Do You Need Help?

Because I know how difficult it is to struggle with five little ones during sacrament meetings, I encourage my eleven-year-old daughter to pick a young mother to assist during every meeting. She brings a bag of toys to entertain the children quietly and has really become a heroine to that young, struggling mother.

Surprise Packages

I wrapped up a little package for each of my children. Their mood was one of eager anticipation until they unwrapped the boxes to find only notes saying "I love you." Their expressions said, "Is that all?" I replied, "There is nothing in this world as valuable to you as being loved. Without love, people's entire lives are void of joy. With it, they can have joy beyond their expectations."

Riddle

I asked my family, "What is one thing that you have to give away in order to receive it in great abundance?" They enjoyed searching for the correct answer, which, of course, is "Love."

PEACEMAKING

"What Do I Do, Mommy?"
If I constantly tell my sons and daughters what *not* to do, but fail to tell them what *to* do, then I'm failing to teach, and I become a negative instead of a positive force in their lives. I try to replace "Don't hit Sissy when she takes that toy away" with "Tell Sissy you'll give it to her when it's her turn, or give her something else that will make her happy."

You Can Handle It
"I know you two children can handle it" is the phrase I use each time I'm tempted to step into their arguments. If the fighting is interfering with my own peace, I isolate them in their rooms.

I Want It
When children argue over who gets the largest piece of cake, let one child cut it into equal portions, then let the other choose the first piece.

Learning Situations
I try to aid my children in perceiving their role or responsibility in a problem or quarrel. They are not allowed

to place blame, but must carefully examine the situation. They must realistically see what happened to recognize their own actions and attitudes. I ask them to tell me how they could have handled the situation differently. In this way, an unpleasant situation becomes a learning experience.

Stop an Argument

Sometimes when children are arguing, I have them stand on opposite sides of a window. They may make faces or say whatever they want, but they can't reach each other. Usually this results in a giggling contest.

Run It Off

Rain or shine, if children are fighting or arguing, I send them for a run around the block or up and down the street. They lose interest in the energy for the fight. When they come back, they have forgotten all about quarreling.

Switch Trick

If children are quarreling, ask them to switch roles and defend the opposite side. They soon stop quarreling.

No More Quarreling!

The most effective method we use to stop quarreling and fighting is to separate the offenders until tempers are cooled. Each child is sent to his own room. We set the timer for five minutes; if they can then discuss the problem without yelling, they may do so. Much of the time, they have forgotten what they were fighting about.

Surprise Compliment

My son and daughter didn't seem to be getting along very well. I decided something needed to be done about it, so I went to each individually and whispered, "Your sister (brother) would be delighted if you did something totally unexpected for her (him). Why don't you try to think of one compliment you could give her (him)? Write it down and we'll wrap it up, along with her (his) favorite candy bar. Then you can sneak it under her (his) pillow tonight." Their happy faces the next morning indicated that it had worked, for that day, anyway. Neither expected to receive from the other!

Biting

If my preschooler bites another child, I have him bite himself just as hard. He learns that it hurts, and he isn't as inclined to do it again. I also say, "Biting is for animals. You're a child of God, so let Heavenly Father see which you want to be."

Who Stirreth Up Anger?

When my children quarrel, I read them this scripture: "He that hath the spirit of contention is not of me, but is of the devil, who is the father of contention, and he stirreth up the hearts of men to contend with anger, one with another." (3 Nephi 11:29.) They don't want to satisfy Satan, so they quickly change attitudes!

Calming Prayer

When contention is in the house, I draw everyone together for family prayer. When we invoke the help of the Spirit, we get it. Sometimes, if the most agitated person offers the prayer, his attitude softens.

A FORGIVING HEART

They Make Erasers, Don't They?

When my son felt overwhelmingly guilty about a mistake, I pointed out that he could erase that mistake through repentance. After all, everyone makes mistakes. Heavenly Father understands. That's why he provided repentance as a way of erasing our errors. They put erasers on the end of pencils, don't they? They wouldn't bother if everyone were perfect.

Repentance

To illustrate the principle of repentance, I showed my children a tarnished piece of silver. I then allowed each in turn to polish a section, until the silver shone brightly. I explained that when we take the steps of repentance, forgiving ourselves and others of weaknesses or wrongdoing, we have polished "tarnish" off ourselves, so that the beauty of purity can shine forth.

Another time I dropped a dirty coin into vinegar to illustrate how, when we go through the process of repentance, we become clean. When the coin comes out, it glistens like new. So do our souls when we repent.

The Lord Gave Men Weaknesses

When my children see weaknesses in others, I tell them that we must look instead for the strengths. Everyone has weaknesses and everyone has strengths. In Ether 12:27, the Lord says, "I give unto men weakness that they may be humble." Who gives us weaknesses? Why? Then should we criticize or ridicule people because they have something the Lord gave them for His own reasons?

What Did Christ Say?

Christ had so much compassion for those who mistreated him that he said, "Father, forgive them; for they know not what they do." (Luke 23:34.) If we can remember those words when we are wronged, we will be stepping toward His perfection.

I Hate Her

Charles Lamb, the English author, once told his friend he hated a man. "But you don't know him," the friend objected. He replied, "Of course I don't. Do you think I could possibly hate a man I know?" When my daughter came to me saying she hated her schoolmate, I told her the above story and told her to look for something in that person that she could praise. The next day, she returned with three positive statements about her. In addition, she began to understand some of the reasons behind the girl's negative qualities. She was getting to know her schoolmate and, with that knowledge, her hatred disappeared.

Helpful Sayings

"Selfishness leads to unhappiness."

"If you think only of yourself, you will dry up inside."

"What you give, you get."

"Love softens the hardest hearts."

"Every ice cube can be melted with the warmth of love."

"Let others feel the rays of your light."

"Look for the good in others. Everyone has something to teach you."

"Always leave people better for having known you."

"To have a friend is to be a friend."

"There are givers and there are takers. Be a giver."

"Any fool can criticize. The wise will compliment."

"Help thy brother's boat across, and lo! Thine own has reached the shore."

2

CULTURE IN THE HOME

If there is anything virtuous,
lovely, or of good report
or praiseworthy,
we seek after these things.
(Joseph Smith, Article of Faith 13.)

A SPIRITUAL RESPONSE

Enrich Sensitivity to Beauty
The purpose of introducing a child to great works of art and music is not merely so that he might acquire a knowledge of the works. It is to awaken or to reawaken his soul to beauty. Children are sensitive, and if we kindle this side of their nature, their life experience will be enriched.

Food, Not Hunger
Before introducing my children to a new painting or piece of music, I tell them that there is a part of their spirit that responds to and loves beauty in all its various forms. In viewing or listening to something beautiful that has lived through the ages, we keep that lovely sensitivity in our natures fed. We wouldn't want it to go hungry, would we?

Example Pays
My husband and I always keep in mind that our children will not enjoy the arts if we ourselves don't.

ART APPRECIATION

Building a Picture Memory

In order to fine-tune my children's memory as well as to give them a mental picture to carry with them wherever they go, I will play a game with them. I'll ask them to study a painting for three or four minutes. Then I will hide it and ask them to recall it. With amazing accuracy, they are able to recall details that I may have missed.

Originals

My children were curious about the location of the original paintings we enjoy so much. A few visits to our local art museum and an explanation about how prints are made from the great paintings hanging in famous galleries all over the world have increased their desire to visit those galleries.

Portrait of His Mother

One day, I found my teenage daughter studying *Portrait of His Mother*, by James Abbott McNeil Whistler, with tears streaming down her cheeks. "She reminds me of that lady we visited in a rest home, Mama. She looks so lonely." I knew that she had experienced an emotional response to the great work. Isn't this one reason Heavenly Father encourages us to seek after these things?

Special Picture Frame

I bought a lovely picture frame with a hinged back at an antique store. It has served the family well, for I will buy a lovely print and place it in the frame. After we've absorbed it for a while, I will change the print. Occasionally I will allow my children the privilege of selecting their own prints.

A Child's Understanding

Although little minds can't understand many technical terms, they can grasp concepts such as color, line, and balance. I will show my young children a painting and ask them questions that point out these concepts, without necessarily using the terms. For example:

1. What colors do you see in this painting?
2. Which one do you see more than the others?
3. Where do you see the color green? In the middle? On the left? On the right?
4. Do you think the artist had a reason for choosing those colors and placing them where he did?
5. How does the color blue make you feel?
6. What shapes do you see on the lady's dress?
7. Do you see that shape anywhere else in the painting?
8. Why do you think the artist put those shapes where he did?
9. What do you see that is little? Big? Medium-sized?

The Gleaners

To illustrate how I help my children see a story in a painting, I'll use the well-known painting by Jean Francois Millet, *The Gleaners*. I'll say to them:

Can you see the three women bending over to painfully pick up every bit of grain that has been left behind by the threshers? They do not want any of the grain to go to waste. Do you think they may be poor people without land of their own?

Ruth, in the Bible, went to Boaz's field to glean the leftover grain. This picture is used often to illustrate that Bible story.

Notice that there are huge stacks of grain in the back of the picture. These have been carefully collected and stacked by the owner of the land. What do you think the man on a horse is doing? Yes, guarding the owner's property, because these sheaves represent many loaves of bread, which would bring him money.

The three peasants are absorbed in searching for the leftover wheat. Their aprons are becoming filled with it, so they will go home with some food for their families. Do you think their children will be happy to see them return?

Curiosity

Many of the Old Masters' paintings touch a sense of curiosity in a child's mind. If he views Velasquez's *The Maids of Honor*, for instance, he will see a little girl in a stiff dress very unlike the clothes of today. Upon investigation, he can learn much about the time of King Philip IV of Spain, whose daughter is represented.

Choice of Art

I have found these rules helpful in choosing art for my children to appreciate:

1. Find pictures with people in action.
2. Choose pictures that have withstood the test of time.
3. Don't present more than one painting at a time.

4. Allow the children's imaginations to soar. Don't tell them they are wrong.

5. Use pictures with vivid colors.

6. Take time to discuss the picture so that the children's understanding will broaden.

7. Don't present factual information about technical details or chronology until the children are mature.

Our Dear Friends

We began slowly collecting prints of fine paintings for our home. Many of them are surprisingly inexpensive. After researching background information about each print and artist, we feel we have graced our walls with dear friends who have stories of beauty to tell us each time we glance at them.

Sketch a Story

When I tell the children a story, I'll often sketch the characters and setting as I'm relating it. For example, if I'm telling the tale of "The Three Bears," I'll draw the woods and the house. Then, as I continue, I'll add the papa, mama, and baby bears. I'll say, "Here is Goldilocks," "Here is the dinner table," and so forth. When the children grow a little older, they will draw their own sketches.

Child's Eye Level

The artwork in my children's room is hung at their eye level, so they can appreciate the pictures without effort.

Blackboard

My children have free access to a chalkboard and chalk from infancy on up. This offers a free arm movement, which is important to budding artists. If a child grasps the chalk too tightly, with tense muscles, I will encourage him to loosen his grip. Even if he only scribbles little lines, I'm content, for I know that if I allow him freedom, those lines will eventually turn into objects.

Picture Gallery

My children have spent many pleasurable hours cutting pictures from magazines and then taping them to their bedroom doors. This is their first art gallery, which is changed as whims dictate.

Shapes Make a Picture

It is important to me that my little girls recognize different shapes. When they are still very young, I will say, "This is a triangle," or "Notice the square." Eventually, they will recognize shapes within objects: "Mommy, the car is really a rectangle." I'll show them how rectangles, circles, squares, and triangles can be turned into a baby carriage, a buggy, a boat, or a car. We sometimes play a game to see what we each draw with the same given shapes.

Tips for Parents

I have found the following guidelines helpful in encouraging my children's love of art:

1. Draw for and with the children.

2. Provide art materials, such as pastels, crayons, finger paints, chalk, and watercolors.
3. Discuss their drawings, listen to their explanations, and exhibit their art.
4. Lift them up to see paintings that are high on the wall, so they can study them.

Release of Emotions

Imagination and emotions are released as a child paints. I never criticize a drawing, because I know it could destroy these important elements. However, I have found that a child can develop a sense of self-criticism that can lead him to improve at his own rate. I will ask one or two questions, such as:

1. What feelings did you have toward the monkey as you were drawing?
2. How did the monkey become green?
3. Why is he up in the air?
4. Does a monkey have one eye?

Story to Tell

I teach my children that pictures have a story to tell. To understand that story, they need to study the clothes of the people depicted as well as the setting surrounding them. We can travel from one century to the next, or from one time or place to another, by viewing a picture.

Our Friends

I try to display paintings that will uplift and inspire my children. They are our friends that we can carry in our minds, wherever we go.

Rent a Painting

Many artists have formed co-ops, where paintings may be rented. Changing the artwork in my home by renting it inspires the children to be curious and interested in it. Often the price of rental may be applied to the purchase price.

Picture Story

I find a picture that can relate to my children's experience in one way or another. Children's books, especially those written at the turn of the century, have lovely illustrations that can be used very nicely for this game. Also, much of the artwork of the Old Masters can be appreciated by even the youngest of children.

One of my favorite pictures is called *The Land of Nod*. In it, over thirty children are climbing a hill in their nightclothes. Some are picking flowers; others are hugging each other. One little boy is leaning against another as if he's falling asleep. I ask my children to study the picture for a few minutes; then I remove it from their sight and they tell me what's in it. After they have described it in great detail, I have them tell me a story about it.

1. Where are these children going?
2. What were they doing before?
3. Why is the one little boy so tired?
4. What was it about the flowers that attracted the ones who are picking them?
5. What will happen to the children when they get to where they are going?
6. How do these children feel right now?

The questions can be endless. However, we should encourage the child to think and be creative. There are no right or wrong answers. Each child can create his own story to his own tastes.

Teach Discernment

Rather than just telling my daughter she did well on a drawing, I try to be specific: "Your choice of colors is very vivid," or "Your lines indicate you have a steady hand."

Continued Picture

Our family sometimes will start a continued picture, to which everyone contributes one part. For instance, someone starts by drawing the roof of a house. The next person adds the base, another the windows, and another the landscaping, until the picture is complete. Even the preschoolers can contribute.

Alternative: Everyone draws a bird by following the leader. The leader says, "This is how you draw the body." Everyone follows his example. "Now, add the head," he says, and so on, until the picture is complete. Little ones can do this step-by-step procedure without difficulty.

Cartoon Contest

We all have humor within us. One way to encourage it wholesomely is to have a family cartoon contest, complete with funny sayings. We used our immediate family as subjects, and the end products were delightfully revealing!

Start with a Line

One person draws a line, or any shape. The next person then must draw something using that line. No one can guess what the picture will be!

Primary Colors

To show the children how mixing the primary colors makes other colors, I soaked sheets of crepe paper in three glasses of water; one yellow, one red, another blue. The water will color nicely in a few minutes. I then took an empty glass and mixed a little yellow with the red. Orange appeared!

The same can be done with yellow and blue to make green, or red and blue to make violet.

MUSIC

A "Hearing Sense"

If a child's sensitivity and natural love of beauty aren't nurtured while he's young, he may lose the sense of appreciation so vital to enriching the soul. A tiny child can learn rhythmic body movements and sing songs by rote. By the time he reaches seven years of age, he should be training his ear to hear different tones, as well as learning the various musical keys and the relationship of one to another. If he will be attentive to a piece of music, he can pick out the pitch, key, timing, rhythm, intervals, and harmony. A patient mother will make this a pleasurable experience by playing listening games with the child:

1. Is the tone high or low, or a combination?
2. What instruments can you recognize? Which one is more dominant than the others?
3. Do you hear anything repeated?
4. Hum the melody.
5. Is it a pleasing tune? How does it make you feel?
6. Clap out the rhythm.

Chant vs. Symphony

Comparing musical pieces has been enlightening to my children. To show the differences in historical growth, I played a simple Gregorian chant and then allowed the children to compare it to the complex structure of Beethoven's Ninth Symphony.

Folk Songs

Music of all nations shows us a vast variety of native rhythms and scale formations. My children can now distinguish the musical characteristics that make an Irish folk song so different from Spanish or Hungarian music.

Composers

I asked one child at a time to pick a composer, read about his life, and listen to his music. He was then to present the information to the rest of the family during family home evening, including a sample of that composer's music. We're growing familiar with the composers and feel an increasing sense of understanding and love for their music.

Play the Cassette

I record classical pieces, such as the *Grand Canyon Suite* or *Peter and the Wolf,* on a cassette tape recorder for my three-year-old. She can operate the machine in her own room whenever she wishes. Even though she's tiny, she has become familiar enough with this music to unconsciously hum it while playing.

Experience It

I play classical music for the children and ask them to close their eyes. They must relax and let the music penetrate their minds. When I turn it off, I'll ask them what they saw and felt. They might describe images or actions that come into their minds. No response is ever wrong. The children's personalities and life experiences are all different—thus, their reactions will differ as well.

Teach Them in Their Youth

I know that the more my children are exposed to excellent music, the more familiar it will become. Their tastes will be refined enough by the time they are teenagers that even though they depart from it for a season, they will return to it.

Rock-A-Bye-Baby

My tiny babies have their first taste of music in the form of lullabies. I sit and rock them to sleep with such songs as Tennyson's "Sweet and Low," Holland's "Rockaby, Lullaby, Bees in the Clover," and Field's "Wynken, Blynken, and Nod."

I want them to hear of Heavenly Father's love and the beauty of life at an early age, so I also sing "Love at Home," "A Mighty Fortress Is Our God," and "I Am a Child of God."

Interpretation

We teach our children to appreciate fine music by having them visualize a story as they listen. To get them started in this process, I will explain the following stories as the pieces are being played, pointing out the different moods and actions as the children listen.

Bach's Invention #1 in C Major. The story is a dialogue between a husband and wife. The wife approaches her husband with a request: "Darling, I would like to redecorate the living room." He answers angrily, "You what? I will not allow it!" The wife tries to persuade him to change his mind, but an argument ensues. It is up to the listener to determine who wins.

Beethoven's Sonata in C Minor, Op. 31. This is a melodrama in which the heroine is being asked to pay the rent or else marry the villain. The villain goes so far as to tie her to the railroad tracks while the train is coming. She, of course, is saved by the hero, just in the nick of time.

Bach's Prelude #1 in C Major. This piece doesn't have a story, but its texture and artistic qualities can be appreciated by relating them to specific character traits. It has a smooth sound like love, strength, majesty, honor, and integrity. As one listens to it or plays it, he should try to feel these qualities within himself.

Perform with the Spirit

I assign my music students to select ten pieces, such as Primary songs or hymns, that would be acceptable for a baptismal service. They practice these pieces for me, contrasting or comparing the qualities in each. This helps the students intellectualize. Then I give them a talk about order and the Lord's sense of time in comparison to ours. I give them examples of what can happen at a baptism if the music does not set the mood. Children become noisy and bored. However, if the musician is in tune with the Spirit, through prayer and faith, he can play his feelings, not just the notes. A spiritual bond can exist between the listener and the music that affects the entire meeting. Whether the child plays well or not, the people are filled with the spirit of the beautiful sounds or feelings. This unites them with a spiritual sense that rises above the notes.

Musical Terms

Do you know the difference between the following terms? We didn't, until we took the time to discuss them in a family home evening. We have also planned to sample each form of art as it becomes available at a nearby college.

1. Opera: A drama that is sung. Uses both instrumental and vocal music.

2. Oratorio: Large-scale musical work with solo voices, chorus, and orchestra, without scenery, costumes, or acting. Has a serious or sacred character, but is not part of a religious service.

3. Symphony: A large-scale work in several parts or movements, for orchestra.

4. Concerto: A large-scale work in several movements, for solo instrument and orchestra. Dramatic tension between the two is built.

5. Sonata: Instrumental work intended for one or two instruments. Has a cycle of contrasting movements, generally three or four.

No Piano

Many families feel limited if they don't have a piano to accompany them in their singing of hymns. The Church Distribution Center now has a set of six cassettes available with organ accompaniment for hymns and ten children's songs (VV0T0529 $8.50.) A small hymnbook is also available. (PMBU0406 35¢.)

Nobody Can Read Music, But . . .

I will often sing hymns while feeding, dressing, and bathing my children. As a result, my children love to sing. Jason, my four-and-a-half-year-old, rides his Hot Wheels bike in our non-Mormon neighborhood singing "We Thank Thee, O God, for a Prophet." This has brought about gospel discussions with my neighbors as well as with my children, giving me rich opportunities to answer questions and define terms. I am not a very good singer, we do not have a piano, and nobody in the house can read music—but that doesn't hold us back!

Singing Instead of Fighting

We have discovered a way to keep the children from fighting while in the car for both short and long trips. We teach them hymns from the "big people's" hymn book, which I carry in my purse at all times. When not driving, I can be free to teach new songs; otherwise, we sing old favorites. I estimate we learn at least two new hymns a month.

A Love for Music

As I was growing up, my father would often tell me to go play the piano while he did the dishes. He would sit for hours and listen to my practicing, encouraging and lovingly offering critiques. He helped me develop a love and reverence for music because of his own love and reverence for it. When music was played or sung in our home, everyone was expected to listen quietly and appreciate it.

Loving Music

To encourage my children to love music, I share it often by doing the following:

1. When they ask a question, I answer in song. "Mom, when can we go swimming?" "Tomorrow, Tomorrow" (song from *Annie*).
2. I allow my children free access to the piano, no matter

how little they are. They "compose" new pieces with great freedom.

3. We play a game of making up new words for old tunes.

4. We play a game of "Guess the tune I'm humming."

5. We imitate the scales with numbers: 1-3-5-3 or 3-5-3-1.

6. I encourage them to sing softly. Harshness spoils the tone.

7. We march to the beat of patriotic songs, alternating marching on tiptoe, then on the heels.

8. I allow them to participate in a "kitchen" band. We use pots for drums and alternate the beat.

9. There is a song suitable for any of life's experiences. If it's raining, I may sing "Singing in the Rain," or if the sun is shining, I may sing "Beautiful Sunshine."

Birds Know How to Do It

"Notice how the birds sing. They open their mouths wide and are relaxed," I will say when a child is singing too loudly or discordantly. I find that changing the tune to light, dainty songs will also help.

Off-Pitch Singer

Just because a child sings in monotone, many people will say he is not musical. I have found that, many times, the problem will be solved when I teach him how to hear the pitch. If he listens carefully to the rise and fall of pitch, he can eventually imitate it with practice. Don't limit the child's musical development by labeling him!

Harmony

A child is capable of picking out the tenor, bass, soprano, and alto singers in harmony, if given the correct guidance. I will show him the difference on the piano and have him try to imitate the sounds.

Influences Nonmember

My nonmember nephew came to stay with us from a neighboring state for a week. While he was here, we sang many Mormon songs. My sister said that she wondered how much Mormon influence he would pick up here, but her question was answered when, as the family traveled in the car, he burst out singing, "I Hope They Call Me on a Mission." Music does influence!

Hum Along

We play short selections of the Masters over and over in our home. We encourage our children to hum along.

Success during Practices

I am determined that my five- and six-year-olds succeed in their music lessons. We practice at the same time every day. To make these sessions fun for them, I have tried the following:

—I reward them after each piece by scratching their backs, getting them a drink of water, or letting them stick a piece of paper ice cream on a cone.

—We laugh together and joke when they make errors, instead of losing patience.

—I award a blue chip for well-played pieces, a red chip for average playing, and a white chip for poor playing. If they get enough blue chips, we'll go someplace special: to a movie, to the park, to the store to buy something, or on a bicycle ride with me.

—I gave them a penny for every piece they played. In the spring, we donated the money to the Primary Children's Medical Center in Salt Lake City.

—We tape-record their songs, and listen to them with joy.

"Do I Have to Practice?"

When my children tire of practicing, I encourage them as much as possible. I've found the following to be helpful:

1. Break up practice time—fifteen minutes before school, fifteen minutes after school.
2. Provide a stool to support the child's feet under the piano. Discomfort may cause distaste.
3. Bring hand sewing into the room and sit with the child as he practices.
4. Encourage the child to memorize one or two pieces. Make requests.
5. Praise! Praise! Praise!
6. Allow the child to play the piece for family home evening or sacrament meeting. A duet with other siblings or with Mom and Dad gives support.
7. Remember, it will improve with time.
8. Pick pieces that interest his age level.

Is It Worth It?

I knew my efforts were worthwhile when my son came home from his mission saying, "Mom, I'm grateful you made me stick to my piano lessons when I was little. I was the only one who knew how to play in the little branch in Holland."

Tiny Performer

I found that my preschooler can perform in sacrament meeting, to the delight of all. I had him play the tone bell while his older sister played "I Am a Child of God" on the piano. If I number the keys and then hold up the number I want him to hit at the right time, he does beautifully.

LITERATURE

A Good Friend

Reading a book is like spending time with a good friend. It converses with me, teaches me lessons, shows me ideals, and pulls forth an emotional response. When I turn the last page over, it's as though I'm saying good-bye to a dear friend.

Universal Emotions

A book becomes a classic because it expresses universal human emotions. Often we have emotions within us that we don't recognize or that we can't express. If we see them in writing, then we are touched and enlightened about ourselves.

Getting Them Started

There are many books that do little to help my children develop into the fine individuals I want them to become. But I've found that if I can interest them in good books, they'll not have an interest in the trashy ones.

After hearing me read aloud one chapter of Dickens's *Oliver Twist*, they were interested enough to read the rest themselves. Since then, I've read aloud the opening two or three chapters of other books, knowing the children will be charmed by the action once the story gets set into motion.

Vocabulary Enrichment

The English language can be beautiful if it is expressed eloquently. I try to encourage my children to read books that are above their vocabulary level, so that their vocabularies are enriched.

Early Introduction

I don't wait until my children are teenagers before I introduce the classics to them. If they become familiar with great books when they are little, they will have the necessary reading and thinking tools to appreciate them when older. (*Bambi, Black Beauty,* and Beatrix Potter's books are examples of classics that younger children can enjoy.)

Expands Experience

I've learned much about history, other countries, and other people through my reading experiences. I know that the worlds my children create within their own minds are enhanced and broadened by their reading experiences.

Read to Them

We love to read to our children, even when they are older. It's a wonderful ice-breaker and aids in reinforcing values.

We Watch What We Read

We know that children are imitators. It would be hypocritical for us to select trash to read, while expecting our children to read uplifting material. There is enough good literature, both inside and outside the Church, to keep us reading for a long time.

Repetition

Books are to enjoy and to love. We encourage our children to read a book over and over again. Each reading increases the understanding and appreciation of the fine character traits and problem-solving portrayed.

Fairy Tales

Fairy tales nourish a child's imagination and often offer wholesome morality. Evil people are defeated, while justice wins. Little minds that need to be nourished are exposed to beauty, goodness, bravery, and heroism.

Appointment at the Library

We have a library visit scheduled for every Saturday. The commitment inspires the desire to read more. If the children are aware of a deadline date, they will be more inclined to finish what they've checked out.

Encouragement

We want our children to discover and develop the joy of reading books, so we encourage them to

—set aside time to read each day.
—give and receive books as gifts.
—visit the library regularly.
—observe Mom and Dad reading.

Book Trade

In order to save money and increase our reading experience, we invited members of our stake to a book-trading potluck dinner. Each family had to bring, along with a dish of food, some discarded books or magazines to trade.

Reading Club

For twenty-five years, a group of mothers has been meeting once a month for reading discussions. They each read one book a month from the classics, biographies, or modern literature.

Bookworms

To motivate our children to read, we have posted bookworms on our family bulletin board, one for each child. Each time a child reads a book, we add a section on the worm, complete with the title of the book.

Comparison

We want our children to develop a taste and desire for good literature, so we allow them to read casual or silly books, as well as those that have endured the test of time. We point out that the quality books use words beautifully and teach valuable lessons about life. When we compare the quality, our children are able to develop their tastes objectively.

Feel the Emotions

One way to learn the scriptures and experience the emotions of the characters is to dramatize a scriptural story. One week one child will write his own script, pick the actors, and costume them, while the next week another child will be in charge. Nephi's experience while being tied up by cruel brothers, or the excitement Joshua felt when fighting the battle of Jericho—these can become vivid if presented in dramatic form. An alternative activity is to present a puppet show.

Family Reading

One evening our family took parts from Shakespeare's *A Midsummer Night's Dream*. We read one scene and enjoyed it so much that we continued with it the next night. Even the little ones appreciated the fanciful characters and rich humor.

Dollhouse

I couldn't understand why my mother brought the dollhouse with all its furniture to family home evening. I should have known she had a lesson in mind! She asked my little sister to be Mrs. Martin Harris and me to be Martin Harris. Dad was Joseph Smith, and Mom played the Lord. We then proceeded to enact in story form how Martin Harris was entreated by his wife to get the translations of the plates from Joseph Smith. I don't think anyone will forget that story now!

Children's Poetry

Children love poetry for its rhyme, rhythm, and meaning. We wouldn't want to deprive them of the opportunity of reading and memorizing such poems as Robert Louis Stevenson's "The Swing," "My Shadow," or "The Land of Counterpane." These each relate to childhood experience and reflect a beauty that inspires.

Incidents in Their Lives

We introduce poetry early by reading it to our toddlers every day. Often we can find a suitable poem to fit an incident or occasion in their lives.

Image of Feelings

Poetry expresses feelings in a way that can perhaps be understood more readily than any other medium. It creates an image in a child's mind that can last forever.

Mother Goose

Mother Goose rhymes are very stimulating to a child's sense of art. They help develop imagination, as animals talk and objects are alive. The rhymes also help memory development.

In Sequence

Always ask children about what they're reading. Have them repeat the story line sequentially. This serves three purposes:

1. You can be sure they're thinking as they read.
2. You show interest in what they're doing.
3. It aids self-expression.

Storytelling

Children love to sit and listen to their mother or father tell them stories. It is not, however, a skill that has come easily to me. I try to follow these rules:

1. Don't make the story too long.
2. Use voice inflections—be excited, sad, angry.
3. Use descriptive words, colors, sounds, smells, and touch.
4. Use your imagination—have objects talk or animals dress crazily.
5. Don't discuss the moral. The story itself will illustrate it.

Repeat Back to Me

My children have certain favorite stories that I encourage them to repeat to me in their own words. If they wish, they may cut pictures out of magazines or even draw their own pictures to illustrate the story. Self-expression is aided and memory enhanced.

Ideas to Cultivate

Families can have fun with stories. We have tried the following ideas in our family:

1. Dress up as a character in a book you have just read. Have the others guess which character you are.

2. Write your own story. Take it to the hospital to be read to sick children.

3. Close your eyes and pretend you are asleep. When you "awaken," relate what you have dreamed.

4. You're going on a trip. You may go anywhere you wish. What is your transportation? What do you see while traveling? Who is there when you get there? What happens to you when you arrive?

SCRIPTURES

Desert Island?

I asked my children what they would take with them if they were to be stranded on a desert island. They each gave different answers, but the one who said he'd take the scriptures was perhaps the wisest. These books contain information about history, success, poetry, wisdom, and, of course, religion. I want my children to value all the books of scripture as the word of the Lord. I stress to them the fact that other religions don't recognize anything but the Bible. Aren't we blessed to have the Book of Mormon, Doctrine and Covenants, and Pearl of Great Price to complement it, support it, and enrich it?

A Little Each Day

After our morning family prayer, I'll read to my children from the scriptures for five to ten minutes. After reading a line, I'll pause to ask for definitions of words or about the actions of the characters. We go slowly, but I know it pays off, because my son recently said, "Mom, I was the only one who could answer the questions in Sunday School because you read to us from the Book of Mormon."

Mirror

My four-year-old said, "I'm going to read the scriptures." He then picked up the volume, flipped to a page at random, and mumbled something. He now goes through this ritual each morning. I've decided that example pays!

Transfer

"You're acting just like Laman and Lemuel!" my six-year-old yelled at her ten-year-old brother. I didn't see what he did to her, but I sensed that she had internalized the meaning of the naughtiness of Nephi's brothers enough to recognize it in her own life.

Scriptures on Tape

We listen to the scriptures on tapes whenever we're in the car.

Scripture Reading for a Six-Year-Old

Soon after my six-year-old learned how to read, he asked, "When am I going to get my own Book of Mormon, like the other kids?" He was ready to begin reading the scriptures! Now we read them for five minutes or so before he falls asleep. It's been delightful to listen to him sounding out difficult words, such as *inhabitants* or *abominations,* and learning the word of God.

TELEVISION CONTROL

World Is Black

When my daughter came to me saying the world was a dark and terrible place, I began to examine why she would be so negative. I found that she had just watched a television program that ended with a teenage girl committing suicide. Upon questioning, I found that this girl had problems to which she could find no other solution than to take her own life. No wonder the world looked black! She wasn't seeing wise solutions to problems.

I then determined to be more closely aware of what my daughter watched. During family council, we decided to schedule TV time each week. Everyone would check the TV log and write down what he desired to watch. Mom and Dad would then approve or disapprove of those desires, keeping total viewing time down to five hours a week for each person.

Pay to Watch

We started charging a ten-cent fee for every half hour of television viewing. We save the money for a family treat night. Since money is valued in our house, television viewing diminished.

Throw the TV Away

We haven't had a television set since we moved into our new home. We find that we play more games together and have much more time to share ideas than we had before. We've even gone on picnics that ended in the family's listening to Dad read the scriptures under the redwood trees. We never would have done that if we had had a television.

Location of the Set

I found that when I move the television set into the kitchen, the teenagers watch less TV, but the little ones watch more. It is the other way around when the television set is in the family room, away from the kitchen activity.

Closet Set

The best place for the television set is in the closet. I can control who watches what because the rule of the house is that no one can bring it out except me.

No Cartoons

If a child watches cartoons before school, he is less likely to settle down to reading in class. As a result, I will allow no TV viewing before school.

Even Exchange

I tell my children that for each hour they play actively, they may watch an acceptable television program. They have found that playing outside is much more fun, and they don't seem to be as interested in the TV programs.

No One Will Watch

If the children quarrel about which television program to watch, I will switch the set off until peace prevails.

Watch with Children

If parents would watch what their children watch on TV, they could make the viewing a learning experience, even if the programs turn out to be negative. The qualities of the characters and the situations they have to handle could become the topics of a lively discussion. Parents could have a chance to explain why one solution or choice may be more beneficial than another.

Old Movies

Some TV reruns, such as *The Brady Bunch, Lassie,* and *Leave It to Beaver* are very good for reinforcing family values. Role models are shown for parents as well as children.

Educational Television

Not all programs are undesirable. Many classics, including Shakespearean plays, are shown on educational television channels. If I am firm and determined to watch such shows, the family will either do something else or join me. Many times they will acquire a taste for these classics because of the exposure to something new.

Send Letters of Thanks

Instead of being grateful for the general conference talks we do receive on television, many Church members complain that we don't receive more viewing time. It would be encouraging if we would send to the broadcasters letters of gratitude and appreciation.

Eliminating Trash on TV

My husband and I have become alarmed with some of the trash on television. We have decided to do the following:

1. Be aware of the content of everything our children watch.
2. Set specific hours of quality viewing.
3. Discuss the programs, characters, and problems the children view, clarifying values and contradicting those that are negative.
4. Join our children in viewing their favorite programs, providing a time of mutual sharing.
5. Plan enticing diversions, such as a family softball game, to get them away from the set.
6. Discuss the commercials, so that the children are aware of the subtle tricks used.
7. Let producers know if we support or dislike programs, and encourage children to write letters.

Quick Quips

"Yes, you have an educational channel on your TV—it's called 'Off.'"

"The box will be unplugged until chores are finished."

"*You* be the boss of the box!"

"You're slipping into a TV trance!"

"Get a balanced diet—turn the channel."

"Television is not a baby sitter."

"What would you have done if you had had that problem in your life?"

3

IDEAS FROM (AND FOR) FATHERS

He shall plant
in the hearts of the children
the promises made to the fathers,
and the hearts of the children
shall turn to their fathers.
(D&C 2:2.)

ENCOURAGEMENT

Creating Self-images

Once I heard a father in the supermarket say, "That was just like you to trip over that can in the aisle." I vowed that I would turn that phrase into a positive one. I say things like, "That's just like you to offer to help with the dishes." "That's just like you to want to give a talk in Sacrament meeting."

My First Time

I'm not ashamed to admit my own mistakes to my children. "After all," I tell them, "this is the first time I've been a father. I'm just learning."

Leave Negative Outside

Before I go home from work, I take an emotional inventory of my feelings. I don't want to take my negative emotional baggage into the house with me, so I prepare myself to greet the family with a happy heart. I think of the eternal perspective, that they are the reason I work, and all those work problems lose their importance.

More than Words

Sometimes a squeeze of the hand, a pat on the back, or a meaningful look conveys more than words.

Priorities

A parent may think he can, but he can't cover up his real feelings or attitudes toward his child. If my heart isn't full of concern for him, he knows it instinctively. I try to keep in focus my priority of being an example, guide, and teacher to my children. In a situation such as my coming home from work tired, I need to remember that rest is important to my body, and I must get enough to restore it, but time spent and patience extended with my children fulfill my eternal goal of bringing my family back to Heavenly Father.

Best for All

Before making decisions, I always ask myself, "What is the best choice for my whole family?"

My Stewardship

I have respect for my children's abilities to make wise decisions. I tell them that I am their steward, that Heavenly Father expects me to give them the tools or principles that will bring them joy. Once they have these principles, they must be held accountable for their own actions. If I failed to give the tools, I would be failing to do my job for Heavenly Father.

Patience

Sometimes, when I become suddenly aware of a spiritual insight that results in a new way of doing something, I am tempted to expect this immediately of the rest of my family, especially my teenagers. It helps to realize that it has taken me forty years to reach this level. To expect my children to be different overnight is useless. Heavenly Father loves me enough to allow me to grow at my own speed. I will allow my children this same experience.

Natural Consequence

As a father, I try to be like my Heavenly Father, who is mucn more interested in my learning what needs to be learned from misbehavior than in punishing. When punishment is necessary, I try to make it fit the crime in natural consequence.

A Safe Jump

My son stands on a chair and then thrusts his body into my arms. He trusts that my arms will be there to prevent him from hitting the floor, bruising his body and causing pain. I've turned this action into a learning experience by relating it to my relationship with Heavenly Father. His arms are there to prevent me from failing the stewardship He has given to me. If I jump in to carry out my responsibilities, He'll be there to help me.

Family Prayer

Whenever I give the family prayer, I try to express my gratitude for each member of the family individually, asking for help in understanding and guiding each in his or her particular problems. For instance, I may say, "Heavenly Father, Susan is not sleeping through the nights. She seems to be so uncomfortable. Please help us discern what is bothering her, and guide us to the most effective solution."

Worthy Goals

As a family, we take all our worthy goals and desires to the Lord. If we need a new piano so that Elizabeth can take lessons, we pray for that goal to be realized. We want our children to see that dreams do materialize with the Lord's help.

Child's Guide

I'll watch my children in their daily activities and ask myself, "What are they feeling right now?" I may guess wrong, but by observing body movements, facial expressions, and actions, I can generally come up with a fairly accurate assumption. This insight aids me in my positive responses to them. I can give a word of encouragement or relate an appropriate experience during the course of the day without directly revealing my insight, or without encroaching upon their sensitivity level.

INTERVIEWS

Father, Consider Your Ways

After watching the filmstrip *Father, Consider Your Ways* (0F090), which can be found in most meetinghouse libraries, I determined to start holding interviews with my children on a regular basis. These are some of the guidelines I have found helpful:

1. Schedule interviews on your calendar on a regular basis. Fast Sunday after church services is the best for me; however, those with larger families may want to see one child each Sunday, or others may find weeknights more compatible to their schedules.
2. Vary the location; you must have privacy! Try holding interviews in a child's bedroom, in a rocking chair, outside on the lawn, on Dad's bed, or while taking a walk around the block, visiting a park, or riding in the car.
3. Open with a prayer. Be relaxed.
4. Be silent for the first five minutes, and just listen.
5. Don't criticize or show any signs of shock.
6. Remember, you are trying to understand the child and open communication.
7. Allow him to snuggle. Physical contact is important.
8. Ask open questions and show genuine interest.
9. Set goals, both long-term and short-term.
10. Discuss problems and solutions. Ask the child what he thinks.
11. Close with prayer.

What Will I Ask?

My husband tries to ask questions that will draw out each child's innermost thoughts. He wants to help them understand themselves, as well as to gain his own insight into them. Some of his questions are:

1. What do you wish your parents would understand about you? Your brother or sister? Your best friend?
2. What advice would you give to someone just joining the Church?
3. If you could change your parents in one way, what would it be?
4. What do you like the least about church? The best?
5. What do you think about when the sacrament is passed?
6. What is your favorite hymn? Why?
7. What would you tell your friend if he wanted you to cheat on a test with him?
8. What made today special for you?
9. If you could have the most perfect parents, what would they be like?
10. How would you change the world if you could?
11. If you could choose to live with a great person from the scriptures, who would it be? Why?
12. Describe a perfect weekend.
13. What is the one thing that makes you most unhappy?
14. What is the best thing about you? The worst?
15. What is your earliest memory?
16. If you could give your mother anything, regardless of the cost, what would it be? Your sister? Your brother? Your best friend?
17. If the house were to burn down, what is the one thing you'd want to save more than anything else?
18. Describe the kind of father/mother you plan to be.

19. What are you proud of yourself for?
20. If you could have three wishes, what would they be?
21. If you had $100 to spend as you wish, what would you do with it?

Interview Myself

Each month before I interview my children, I give myself a "temple-recommend interview." I let my children know there are many things that I need to improve upon and that improvement is a lifelong pursuit.

Dad, I Need an Interview!

I knew that I finally was making progress with personal interviewing when my nine-year-old son said, "Dad, I need a PPI, quick!" He had thrown a firecracker into the backyard, and the yard had caught on fire. He wanted to quickly settle the matter with me before anyone else told me. That is the open communication I hope to maintain.

Patriarchal Blessing

Our stake patriarch maintains that a child should get his patriarchal blessing when he is ready for it. If he knows he wants it and is worthy for it at age ten, then there's no reason to wait. The blessing can be an aid to the parent if he knows the child's weaknesses as they are stated in the blessing, and it can also be a constant reminder to the child, with the parents' help, that he has great potential. This knowledge can be very comforting during the crucial middle years before adolescence.

Goal Setting

Once a month, during our interviews with Dad, we each fill in the following contract. When it is complete, we hang it as a constant reminder on our bedroom bulletin board or bathroom mirror. Dad rewards us upon completion of the goal with a trip to an ice-cream parlor. (Even Mom and Dad fill one out!)

Goal-Setting Contract

On this ____ day of ____________ in the year of
day month

________, I, ______________________________, being of
year your name

sound mind and body, do hereby promise to achieve

______________________ by ______________________
goal specific action

on or before ______________________.
date of completion

____
Witnessed by

____
Signed by

Storybook Interview

We have an office in our home in which I conduct my bishop's interviews. My four-year-old daughter approached me and said, "Dad, can I have an interview?" I invited her in, and as soon as she was sitting still on the chair facing me, she said, "What story will you tell me?" She thought that was what an interview consisted of. I let her choose her favorite story.

I Need to Improve

My father presents the following chart to us during our interviews with him in order to help us improve ourselves. After we fill it in, he allows us to choose an area in which we need to improve. We promise to work on it until the next interview, at which time he will ask for an accounting of it and help us to choose another. In this way, we feel we are successfully growing each month. (Chart is adapted from *New Testament Student Manual,* 1975, p. 10.)

The Commandment	My Performance	
	Satisfactory	Needs Improvement
1. I pray morning and night, not just as a habit, but as a talk with a friend.		
2. I obey the Sabbath. I enter into the Lord's presence, and I refrain from doing my own pleasure.		

The Commandment	My Performance	
	Satisfactory	Needs Improvement
3. I attend church and other activities regularly.		
4. I fast. It brings me joy.		
5. I pay a full tithe. I give freely of my means to build up the kingdom.		
6. I am morally clean.		
7. I am living the Word of Wisdom.		
8. I help our family have family home evenings.		
9. My life-style is within Church standards in: manner of dress language music entertainment dancing		

The Commandment	My Performance	
	Satisfactory	Needs Improvement
10. I read the scriptures daily.		

Personal Commitment

In my first interview with my dad, he presented the following commitment to me to consider and then sign in his presence, if I desired. It now hangs framed in my bedroom as a constant reminder to me of my commitment to my Heavenly and earthly fathers. I plan to take it to college and then have it hanging in my own home someday.

A Personal Commitment

"I accept the challenge of this unique era in which the Lord has allowed me to live. I dedicate myself to the belief that God has a work for me to do and assert that I shall exert the full energy of my soul in accomplishing that work.

"I commit myself without reservation to the laws and principles of the gospel, that through my obedience I might step from the ranks of the commonplace and distinguish myself as one of the faithful and valiant among the sons and daughters of God.

"I shall, from this day forth, strive continually to increase my faith in Christ, that the spiritual powers and direction that flow from this gift might be mine to enjoy in their fulness.

"This pledge I make in and of my own free will, not as a means toward achieving the honor and praise of others, but as a witness of my love for the Father, as well as my determination to fulfill the stewardship he has given me to perform."

(*New Testament Student Manual*, 1975)

AT THE DINNER TABLE

I Remember When . . .

Occasionally I will recall an incident in the life of one of my children while we're eating dinner. "I remember when we were waiting for the arrival of a new little child. The one I'm thinking of came on a rainy night a little faster than we anticipated—in fact, I ended up delivering it right in the back seat of the old Volkswagen . . ." They love hearing stories about themselves, and it reaffirms our love for them.

Happy Thought

Each member of the family is told to bring a happy thought to the dinner table. We will then share their thoughts, one by one. No negative thoughts or worries are allowed. If anyone has a problem or a negative feeling, he is expected to discuss it privately with Dad before retiring.

Spreading Happiness

At the dinner table, Dad will ask one child what another one at the table did to bring happiness into the family. The answers range from "I saw John tie Jeff's shoes for him this morning" to "Mom took a loaf of bread to the neighbors." They all must be positive. Everyone tries to please the others all day long, because no one knows what Dad will ask.

Brain Power

At the dinner table, Dad will often ask one question that will cause great speculation and may send everyone to the encyclopedias or scriptures for an answer. Some of his questions may be:

—How does a dog recognize a stranger?
—What is the difference between a robin and a crow?
—What happened to the Ark of the Covenant?
—What is a *sheum?* (See Book of Mormon.)
—What makes us sneeze?
—Why does a duck remain dry?
—What is Idumea? (See Doctrine and Covenants.)

Who Will Bless the Food?

On weekdays, Dad selects the person who says the blessing on the food. Even the two-year-old is given the honor. However, on the Sabbath, it is always Dad's turn to offer the blessing. He holds the priesthood and is the head of the house, and this is our way of letting him know we honor him just as we do our Heavenly Father on the Sabbath.

Solving Dinnertime Hassle

My children seemed to always want Mom's and Dad's attention when we were exhausted and anxious to get dinner out of the way. We decided that one night a week—besides family home evening—would be devoted to them. We either pack a picnic or order pizza or deli sandwiches. Then we go to a park, where the kids play contentedly until bedtime. They love it and are quite ready for bed with no fuss when we arrive home.

MAKING MEMORIES AT BEDTIME

Candlelight
When I started telling the children bedtime stories by candlelight, I thought they might be frightened. Instead, it added a warmth to the moments shared with me.

Race for Bed
In order to get my preschoolers to bed quickly, I have them run a race to try to beat their previous time getting into bed. They go quickly when I start to count, "One, two, three . . ."

Robot Ride
Dad is a robot. The children sit on his shoulders. Two taps on his head tell him to go forward, One taps means to stop. A tug on the right ear means to go to the right, and a tug on the left ear means turn left. The natural destination is, of course, bed.

Personal Stories
Dad makes up stories about each of the children. "SuperJohn" might be the hero, while "Lucy is just your age." Everyone feels that the story is special, just for him.

Dad Reads

My husband is the one who reads to the children. He will read the *Friend* magazine to them, and they love it! It gives me a few quiet moments to myself or with the baby during those hectic hours after dinner and before bedtime.

Who Loves Me? Who Loves You?

I say, "Who loves me?" The reply is, "I do." Then I say, "Who else?" My child gives names. I say, "Who loves you?" "You do." "Who else?" I help him to think of every person who touches his life, ending with Heavenly Father and Jesus. This has become our special nightly ritual.

Discuss Tomorrow Tonight

I am not with the small children at the beginning of the day because I leave the home at 5:30 A.M. I try to make it up to them by "starting their day" with them before bedtime. Each child gets one story, prayer, and quiet "alone" time to discuss the day and the goals of tomorrow.

"Good Night, Dad"

After baths, my husband tucks our older children into bed, one at a time, spending ten minutes listening to each tell about his day. This way they have Dad's undivided attention, and Mom has time to rock the baby to sleep.

"I Want to Be near You"

When one of our children is ill and needs nighttime attention, I bring the chaise longue in from outside, and he sleeps near me during the night. It is also a portable bed during daytime illness. It can be propped up if a child has congestion.

JUST FOR FUN

Magic Carpet Ride

Dad invites one child at a time onto his bed for a magic carpet ride to different countries. Dad will give him a pretty blue stone with a hole in it, which he calls a talisman. After rubbing the talisman three times and making a wish to go to a country of his choice, the child must close his eyes and hang onto the "magic carpet." If he goes to Holland, for example, Dad will paint a word picture of people wearing wooden shoes and a land dotted with windmills.

Shaving Partners

When six-year-old Johnny gets up early enough, my husband will ask him to join him at the sink to be his "shaving partner." Johnny will lather up just like Dad and then "shave" with an old, blunt butter knife.

Saturday Trade

Sometimes Dad needs a Saturday alone with Mom, so he will trade a Saturday of fun with another father. One Saturday he will have all the children for a day at the zoo, or a bicycle repair lesson, or whatever else he wishes to do with them. The next Saturday he will be free because the other father will have the children.

Take Toys Apart

When my children outgrow a toy, I give them a screwdriver and let them take it apart in order to explore the design. Clocks, radios, and computers with broken parts can also delight a child.

Prepared for Nature Trips

I take the children on many outdoor activities. In order to be prepared, I keep several books in the car with information on wild flowers, birds, trees, shells, rocks, or land formation. When we see something new, we look it up and discuss it. I also keep a roll of plastic bags in case the children want to take something home for collections.

Using Tape

My husband has put the tape recorder to use in a number of ways, such as these:

1. Each child finds a tape of his favorite songs under his pillow.
2. Bedtime stories are recorded in Dad's voice to help little ones feel Dad's presence.
3. With the children, a radio program is created, complete with commercials. "This Is Your Life" could be recorded if someone needs honoring.
4. Each child is encouraged to record his day's activities.
5. A letter is taped to send to grandparents or a missionary.
6. Genealogy information is recorded for a child. "I remember when Grandma Smith . . ."
7. A love message is left for child when Dad is gone.
8. A child is given a blank tape to record his or her message for Daddy to listen to on the way to work.

Roughhousing

My little boys look forward to their daddy's time at home because he will roughhouse with them for five or ten minutes. He will lie "dead" on the floor, expecting them to find the right tickle spot to wake him up. They may find it immediately, or they may have to tickle one spot and then another until he finally comes to life with a laugh or giggle. At that moment, they run away, because he'll catch them and tickle them in return.

Monster

Dad plays "monster" with us. We try to get away from him without his catching us and tickling us. He growls until he gets us.

"Splish Splash"

When we were in a swimming pool, my daughter suggested, "Dad, let's have a balancing contest." She climbed up on his legs as he sat on the steps. Balancing herself with one foot on his left leg, the other on his right, she would count until she fell backward into the water. Her brothers would then try to beat her time. With all the giggling, I could understand why my children love their dad!

Field Trips with Dad

My husband will take one of our children with him when he does errands on Saturday. Each one looks forward to his day with Dad, even the teenagers. Depending upon the age, Dad will stop off at the:

—fire station
—print shop

—bakery
—airport
—pet shop
—building site
—park
—football practice
—antique store
—home teaching

One baker makes it a habit to give the child a dime each time he comes. It's delightful to find that so many shopkeepers are willing to show the child around.

If he has time, Dad will ask the child to write a book about his "field trip." The young child dictates to him what he wishes to say, and then draws a picture. It may be many pages or just one, depending upon the interest. If we photocopy the little book, we then have a copy to send to grandparents and one for his Book of Remembrance. The original can be used by the child to read each night before falling asleep.

"Do-It-with-Dad" Jar

Our children brainstormed all the activities they enjoyed doing with Dad. They then wrote them on slips of paper and placed them in a "Do-It-with-Dad" jar. The activities couldn't be time-consuming or expensive, just fun! We draw one each time we have a family council and then schedule it for later that week. Some ideas we included are:

—Take a bicycle ride.

—Go on a penny hike. Flip a coin. Heads means turn right; tails, turn left.

—Go to ice cream store for cones, or make fresh ice cream.

—Play a game of softball, football, or badminton.

—Watch special TV movie, snuggling with Dad.

—Have Dad be a slave for fifteen minutes for each child.

—Have Dad be in a contest against you: jumping rope, doing sit-ups, jogging, smiling, eating candy bars, not talking.

—Rock with each child in rocking chair for ten minutes.

—Look through Dad's yearbook, and listen to his childhood stories.

—Take a nap with Dad outside on a blanket, or sleep overnight.

—Work on Scouting skills with Dad.

—Plant garden.

—Enjoy an on-the-lawn picnic lunch or supper prepared by Dad.

—Play "Indians" with Dad. He's the chief. Build teepee with a blanket. Listen to Indian tales, and wear costumes made from crumpled grocery sacks.

—Go on nature hike and identify birds, trees, and wild flowers. The local federal Fish and Wildlife Service can tell you where nearby nature trails are located.

—Go to the zoo.

—Go out for Saturday breakfast.

Anti-Boredom Box

Dad packed an "Anti-Boredom Box," made from an old tackle box, in the car when we went on our family vacation. Each day of the trip we were allowed to dig into the box for a new treasure. This is what we found:

—Gum

—Puzzles and crosswords

—Old copies of the *Friend* magazine

—Book of riddles

—Note pads

—Wallet (used), filled with old pictures and credit cards

—Book of camp songs
—Crayons and coloring books
—Food: candy bars, potato chips, fruit, marshmallows
—An old clock (Twisting knobs or learning how to tell time can keep a preschooler happy)

Travel Pillowcase Cover

When we travel, each child has his own pillowcase cover. Mom embroidered our names on ours, but you could also simply choose a different color for each child. Either way, everyone can easily identify his own pillow, thus preventing conflict.

Car Games

The following are some games we like to play in the car:

1. License Plates. See who can spot the most out-of-state plates.
2. Alphabet. Watch the signs for ABCs in order. One person spots an A. Everyone then looks for B until someone finds it, and so forth.
3. Geography. Name a place that begins with the last letter of the place just named; for example, (1) California, (2) Alaska, (3) Arkansas, (4) South Carolina.
4. Animals. Play a scoring game as follows: For every dog seen, score one point, three points for each cat, ten points for every sheep or horse.
5. Numbers. Add several numbers in your head, subtracting some as you go along. One person dictates, and others try to be the first with a correct answer.
6. Guess. What time will it be when we arrive at the next town? How many miles will we travel before seeing another gas station? How much gas will we use this day?

Trade Roles

"You be the dad and I'll be the child," my husband will say to the children. He then will do everything they tell him to do. He learns just how they view him.

Use Your Imagination

Dad will sometimes say, "What if . . ."

—your best friend wanted you to run away with her?

—you didn't have to go to school anymore?

—you could jump on an airplane and go anywhere you wished?

—you were being teased by your friends about being a Mormon?

—you lost your eyesight?

MAKING MEMORIES WHILE AWAY

An Extra Kiss

Whenever my father would leave when I was small, he would gently kiss the palm of my hand and then wrap my fingers into a fist. He would tell me that I would always have an extra kiss waiting, should I need one.

She Started to Smoke

When my father was busy as bishop, my sister rebelled by smoking. When he discovered her self-destructiveness, he let his counselors take over for him for a while, so that he would have time to be with her constantly. She felt his love and concern for her, and she soon stopped her newly acquired habit. Somehow we knew his love and concern for us was greater even than for his calling as bishop.

Keeping Track

One father keeps at work a copy of the time schedule of each member of his family, so that he can keep track of the hourly activities of each. It helps him to remember that, if teenager Jim has a test at 11 A.M., he could support him through prayer at the specific time his son needs it.

"I Care"
My husband is very busy, but he is never too busy to call home from work for a brief moment. He makes a point of speaking to one child at a time about one thing that is important to that particular child. Sometimes, however, he doesn't have any more time than to say, "I want my little Honey Bear to know I love her."

Tic-Tac-Toe with Dad
One day my four-year-old received a letter from Dad in the mail, while Dad was at work. In it was a tic-tac-toe board with one square marked with an "X." My son marked an "O" in another square, and we mailed it back to Dad's office. Each day he anticipated the mail with delight until the game was over.

Dad, Where Are You?
Because my husband travels in connection with his business and also has time-consuming priesthood responsibilities, his time with the children is limited. He knows they need his attention, so he will often send them postcards or leave little notes or gifts behind to be opened each day he is away. He varies his approach, so they never know what to expect. When possible, he will take a child with him when he travels. Each knows his turn will come eventually.

Reminder for Dad
If one of our children receives a Scouting award or achieves excellence on a school paper, I ask him to leave it by Dad's pillow or dinner plate, so that we don't forget to share it with

him. Sometimes we have the children keep a special "I-Did-It" book for Dad, which explains their thoughts about the activities they've been involved in while Dad was away.

Leave an Influence Behind

Before our father leaves for several days, he gives each of us a charge to maintain the household in one way or another. He varies them each time, but we all feel very responsible, because we know he'll ask for a report when he returns. Sometimes he will give each of us a blessing. We know we come first in his life.

A PRACTICAL SOLUTION

Touch and Feel
Children enjoy feeling different textures of materials. I covered a wooden board with contact paper, and then glued to it such materials as yarn, feathers, velvet, and plastic. These materials can be changed as desired.

Auto with Gadgets
Our children will play for hours in the "automobile" Daddy made for them. Attached to the "instrument board" are such gadgets as old alarm clocks, dials of thermometers, snap locks, and anything else that a child might tinker with.

Large Refrigerator Boxes
Large refrigerator boxes that Dad painted can be used by children as playhouses, ships, rockets, covered wagons, or anything the imagination can conjure up.

Bulletin Board Wall
My teenage daughter kept putting holes in the walls of her room with nails for hanging awards, posters, and pictures on. I decided to cover the entire wall, floor to ceiling, with bulletin-board cork. For those children who have collections, shelves can be made to cover the walls.

Growth Chart

I painted a growth chart on the bedroom wall for my preschoolers. The girls have flowers lined up the wall, while the boys have animals.

Chalkboard Door

Every child needs a chalkboard at his disposal. I used chalkboard spray to spray the back of my children's bedroom door. Now they can use it endlessly.

What Is Your Job?

A first-grade teacher once told me that she was concerned about the fact that many of her students had no idea what their fathers did for a living. Many of those who knew their dads' titles, such as stockbroker or salesman, didn't know what those terms meant. One child thought a stockbroker sold stockings! This teacher asked the fathers to take their children with them to work, if possible. If not, showing the child pictures of Dad on the job and offering simplified explanations of the work he does can allow for a deeper understanding—strengthening the bonds between father and child.

Follow My Example

To encourage our children to keep their rooms neat and tidy, I have relieved my wife of the responsibility of making our bed and tidying our room. I tell the children that, if they find my room untidy in the morning, they can leave theirs untidy as well. However, as long as mine is neat, theirs must also be neat.

Time to Assess

When I find myself car pooling, I try to use the time wisely. I may plan my goals or work on assessments for the children.

Fire Drill

I have a plan of escape for my family in case of fire or other disasters. Everyone knows what route to take and where to meet when he hears the smoke alarm. Occasionally I'll set it off when they least expect it. We've been able to practice our plan and perfect it over the years.

Hands Up

After accidentally slamming one child's fingers in the car door, I now have this rule: As soon as everyone is in, I shout, "Hands up!" The children put their hands behind their heads, and the doors are safely shut.

Seven Syllables

I teach my children to remember phone numbers by singing seven notes that are familar to them. Putting the numbers to the seven notes of a tune, such as "Mary Had a Little Lamb," makes it easy to recall.

Red Washcloths

I keep a few red washcloths in the closet with the first-aid supplies. When I wash off a bleeding sore with one of these, the child is not so frightened as he might be of the blood.

Sand in the House

After continued complaints about sand from under the swing being tracked into the house, I purchased a large square of turf grass to place under the swing. It works very well. Indoor-outdoor carpet would be a fine alternative.

Knobs on Puzzles

To make it easier for little hands to use the more inexpensive wooden puzzles, I purchased small, unpainted furniture knobs and glued them on with permanent bonding glue. They are easily painted to match the picture. These puzzles also make good gifts.

Bath Time

After enduring much screaming at shampoo time, my husband suggested a headrest for the children to lean back on. We fill a large plastic bag or jug with water, and the child uses it as a neck support during shampoos.

TRIBUTES

Crazy Camp-out

One of my dearest memories is of the time Dad took us camping. We failed to find an adequate spot, so we ended up sleeping on the tables in a picnic rest-area shelter. Crazy, but I'll never forget it. We laughed together about our "camp-out" for years afterward.

Treated Like a Queen

From the earliest time I can remember, my father taught me that I deserved to be treated like a queen or princess. He always helped me on with my jacket, opened the door for me, and taught my brothers to let me go first through the door. I knew I had to marry someone who would treat me as well.

A Source of Joy

No matter what I did with my father, he always gave me a feeling that he enjoyed being with me. He'd often grin and tell me, "I had fun." I felt that I was source of joy to him.

Took Time to Understand

My dad always took time to find out what I was thinking. I'd never have the desire to keep it from him, because, I learned quickly, he always gave me wise counsel. Then he let me choose whether to follow it or not.

Love for Grandmother

My husband was describing his deceased grandmother, whom the children had never met. He choked up with tears, and everyone could instantly feel his deep attachment for her. Hearts were filled with a serene feeling of love for her.

Favorite Child

When I recently saw my grown brothers and sister, I told them I had a confession to make that I had never before revealed. They listened intently when I told them that I felt I was the favorite child in my family. We were all amazed, because each said that he or she felt the same way. My parents really knew how to make us feel special.

"Now, Let Me Tell You . . ."

My father used to embark upon lengthy explanations that could easily have been called lectures. I remember tuning him out and just praying silently for them to end. Now that I have my own children, I find myself wanting to lecture in the same way. I remind myself, "Remember, all you will teach them is how to tune you out." Now I ask them questions that will lead them to the conclusion my lecture would have tried to reach:

"Daddy, may I ride my bike to Jimmy's house?"

"On one condition. Do you know what it is?"

"I know—to obey all the rules and get back by dinnertime."

"That's right. Can you tell me what the rules are?" and so on.

4

A HOUSE OF ORDER

Organize yourselves;
prepare every needful thing;
and establish a house,
even a house of prayer,
a house of fasting,
a house of faith, a house of learning,
a house of glory, a house of order,
a house of God.
(D&C 88:119.)

ORGANIZE YOURSELF

A Plan
The first thing the Lord did when he created the earth was to make a plan. Then, step by step, He gathered and ordered materials to form the universe. He wants us to be just as thoughtful and diligent in our own material worlds over which we are stewards. Without a plan and step-by-step course of action, we are limiting our usefulness.

Masters
Physical chaos does not bring peace of mind or true happiness; it can indeed block progress. It keeps us ruled by the material instead of by the spiritual. We become slaves to our worldly possessions, not masters over them, if we fail to organize them.

Freedom
I found that as I put forth the effort to become more organized and get rid of the clutter in my home, my mind also became less cluttered.

A Whole New Start
Periodically, when I see that my whole home needs reorganizing, I will set aside three to four days, pay a

babysitter to take the children, and work straight through until everything looks brand new. I figure that my time, without children's interruptions, is worth the money spent.

A Little at a Time

When our home needs a new start, I (1) assess the situation, (2) break each room down (one at a time) into one- or two-hour segments, and (3) whittle away at it (one closet, three drawers) until the whole house is orderly again.

I keep enough boxes with me for sorting as I go, so that at the end of the allotted time, I can stack them neatly away, ready for continued use tomorrow.

Positive Reinforcement

It used to be difficult for me to make myself keep things up. I find that when I'm having difficulty maintaining my goal of being organized, it's helpful to repeat these two sayings to myself several times a day:

1. "The reason I am ordering my life is for me, for my peace of mind, my own convenience, for the new time and energy I feel flowing through me each time I pay the price. In choosing to be organized, I am choosing true freedom."
2. "I have a new desire for a more orderly way of life. I am choosing this because of *my* own desires and *my* own goals for my family."

My Biggest Help

Prayer is such a source of strength to me. I know that my Heavenly Father wants to help me get my life in order. He doesn't want outside forces running my life. He wants me to succeed, and He is there supporting me when I ask. His words comfort me: "Trust in the Lord with all thine heart; and lean not unto thine own understanding. In all thy ways acknowledge him, and he shall direct thy paths." (Proverbs 3:5-6.)

My Own Way

The only person I have to please in terms of what being organized means is myself. I first have to accept me and my own definition of organization. No "how-to" book has had the complete answer. As soon as I know what is important to me, rather than to others, I am ready to start.

It's Our House

After years of badgering my husband for not being willing to help keep the house up to my standard, I finally said, "Let's decide how *we* want the house." Now that we have decided together what level of order to maintain, much of the tension between us has eased.

"Do It"

After years of rationalizing that some people were just "born unorganized," I discovered, much to my dismay and enlightenment, that everyone who enjoys the peace of a well-run, organized home really does pay the price. They may appear to have some secret abilities; however, even though they may enjoy doing it more, they still have to *do it!*

Throw Aways

When deciding whether or not to save an item, ask yourself:

1. Have I used it in the past year?
2. Does it have real monetary value?

3. Does it have much sentimental value?

Throw away if there are two "no's." If there's any doubt, throw it out. Chances are you won't be sorry. If you are—buy a new one!

Risking

When I find myself resisting the job of consistently delegating and following through with my children's training, I think of Heavenly Father and how He delegates our earthly work to us. He reminds us of our commitments and the possible consequences should we fail; then He lets go. There's risk involved—risk of imperfection that every *good* parent must take.

Super-Mom Myth

Many "Super Moms," those who do it all, are just that because they've never learned the art of delegating household duties to various members of the family. When we're in a hurry to get something done, it's much easier for most of us to do it ourselves—but what a disservice to the children's developing characters! In delegating, I have found the following to be helpful:

1. Heavenly Father expects the children to be taught and trained to be doers, not spectators.
2. Let go of your need for perfection. Well-trained children will pay off greater dividends in the long run.
3. Detach yourself emotionally; walk away, so to speak, once you've trained and assigned the job to someone else. Don't yield to irritability or anxiety.
4. Follow through with the check-up on quality and completion of chores.
5. Don't delegate just the "janitor" work. Include the "fun stuff" too.
6. Reward with praise and acts of thoughtfulness.

ORGANIZE YOUR HOME

Baskets
I keep a decorative basket near my kitchen sink. Into this, I put any small items left in the kitchen area, such as pencils, clips, letters, or small toys. I take these out and organize them periodically, but meanwhile, the basket serves as a functional attractive addition to my room.

I also use a small, pretty basket to hold napkins for the dinner table.

Going, Going, Gone
When I am feeling overwhelmed with the collection of pots, pans, dishes, and other clutter in my kitchen, I box everything up (except daily necessities) and take it to a convenient place in the garage. For the next six weeks, I bring in items only as needed. At the end of this time, I have dramatically narrowed the number of items in my kitchen. Those things that are left are the ones I really use, and they are much more accessible.

Recipe Cork
Glue the top half of a cork to the top of your recipe file; it holds recipes upright while you're cooking.

No Smudge
Spraying recipe cards with hair spray will help keep them clean.

End of Towel Search
To solve the problem of matching the colored towels with their proper bathrooms, I use a solid neutral color such as beige, brown, or gray for walls, shower curtain, window curtains, and throw rugs. Then I can use an unlimited selection of interchangeable colored towels for accent. All my towels now can be used in any bathroom, and I can change the accent color according to my whim.

Double Duty
I use my children's bathing time to clean my bathroom. I have to be there anyway, and it really saves time.

"I Can't Reach"
Use a small step stool for toddlers at the sink to encourage independent tooth brushing and washing.

Play to Clean
When my children need an extra scrub to get dirty little hands clean, I give them a sponge or rubber doll with a bar of soap. With the amount of bubbles this produces, they are clean in no time.

Grooming Boxes
My children have their own personal grooming boxes, which we stack neatly at the end of the bathroom counter. Each box

holds a brush, comb, toothpaste, deodorant, and other accessories for that child. No one is ever permitted to get into another child's supply. On the back of the bathroom door is a pad and pencil to list replacement needs and purchases.

Hang It Here!

I had my husband hang a small painted ladder on four hooks from my laundry room ceiling. It works wonderfully to hold anything that needs hanging until it's put away.

Laundry Pay-Off

I've found that if I truly pay the price to keep up with my laundry on a semiweekly basis, I save both money and time.

1. We need fewer clothes. (Five good interchangeable outfits are enough. It also takes less drawer space to put things away.)
2. I lose fewer items.
3. There is always something to wear.

Mismatched Socks

I have a special drawer in the laundry room where I deposit all unmatched socks. Every week or so, I will pay a child who needs extra money five cents a pair for sorting and matching.

White Socks, Etc.

To get socks and other clothing white:

1. Presoak in baking soda and water before washing.
2. Boil in water and add lemon juice or water mixed with cream of tartar before wash.
3. Use a liquid bleach.

4. When you have really dirty clothes, add a little ammonia to the wash water.

5. Erase make-up from collars and clothing with white bread before washing.

6. Cover the marks on a white collar with white chalk.

7. To remove grass stains from pants, sponge alcohol onto the stain before laundering.

Turntable Make-up Tray

My teenage daughter found an old turntable (the kind that is used in kitchens for dishes and spices) and sprayed it a bright color to use on her dresser top for her make-up. Now she keeps everything in one place and easily accessible.

Toy Scoop

To encourage my children to put their toys away, I keep two clean, plastic dustpans in with their toys. They can quickly scoop up toys and small blocks with these. Often they will each take a dustpan and have a contest to see who can get the most scoops.

"That's Mine!"

Each of my children has his own art supply box. I cover shoe boxes with contact paper, using a different design for each child. I wrap strips of the same paper around his scissors, crayons, watercolors, glue, and pencils. This has eliminated many "that's mine" hassles.

Crayon Reinforcement

To keep crayons from falling through the bottom of the crayon box, wrap masking tape around the bottom for reinforcement.

Storing Small Toys

The following are useful for storing small toys:

—Shoe boxes covered with contact paper and labeled.

—Fishing tackle boxes.

—Grapefruit bags with woven drawstrings.

—Small suitcases.

—Plastic dish drainers for coloring books, records, or paper. The silverware portion is perfect for crayons and pencils.

—Vegetable bins, which keep toys visible.

—Washtubs.

—Large laundry baskets.

—Mesh drawstring bags, sold at camping stores.

—Plastic or tin wheat buckets.

—Plastic garbage cans.

—A large fish net for scooping up bath toys and hanging over shower.

—Restaurant supply jars.

ORGANIZE YOUR CHILDREN

My Child Is My Student

I view life as a school. Heavenly Father has sent me here. He has prepared my curriculum, and I can advance as far and as fast as I am willing to learn. At home, I have the opportunity of being my children's prime teacher for a certain number of years. How my children respond to this school of life—how far they will advance and whether or not they will be good teachers themselves—depends upon the quality of my teaching. I spend a good deal of time in my children's formative years helping them understand their responsibilities and helping them see that we must work together for the degree of order we maintain. I see to it that each child has specific things that must be done every day. It doesn't really matter that there are certain days when they grumble. I also make them do some things that would be easier for me to do myself, because *they* need to learn, not I.

Investment Opportunity

I think that spending the time necessary to train my children well in assuming household responsibilities is the best investment in the future I can make. The payoff for taking the extra time now will be added free time as they assume more and more of the responsibility. It really would be easier and less time-consuming to do everything myself when they are small, but the toll on my future time with selfish, spoiled, untrained children would be great.

One Week at a Time

At family home evening, as we were discussing how to better organize our home, we decided to pay particular attention to one problem area each week. We made a sign holder to hold each week's goal. For example, this is "no-dishes-on-counter" week.

Equal Opportunity

We run an "equal-opportunity" home. Every member helps equally, including Dad and big brothers.

The "Big Three"

At our home, the code word is "Big Three." Each morning, before coming to breakfast, everyone must have completed three things:

1. Have bed made and room tidy. (They do this before leaving bedroom.)
2. Brush teeth.
3. Dress. (We set the clothes out the night before.)

The children memorize these tasks as 1, 2, and 3. This eliminates the necessity of having them on the daily chart. The other tasks are waiting on our revolving chore list.

Teach Them to Do It Themselves

I try not to be too quick to help my preschoolers do things they can do for themselves, such as dressing. Each time, I will explain softly how to do it, giving them an opportunity to try it themselves. As soon as I feel they're properly trained, I will step back to let them do it alone. They are so proud of their accomplishments.

Curing the Slowpoke

My son was not getting ready for school on time. I found myself pushing and pulling to get him out the door to catch the bus. We solved the problem by having him keep track of his efforts with a simple chart posted on the refrigerator door.

He was to awaken one hour before departure time. One check would be placed on the chart for "make bed," "get dressed," "comb hair," and so on. Twenty minutes before departure time, he was to be seated at the table ready for breakfast. His books and jacket were to be near the door. If the checks weren't on the chart, and if he wasn't ready to leave after breakfast, he would lose a privilege.

I found that setting a timer and having him try to beat his previous time helped him to see how quickly those things could be accomplished.

No Dress, No Eat

I never serve breakfast to any child who still has his pajamas on. He must be dressed and have his hair combed if he wants to be admitted to the breakfast table.

Eight-Year Alarm

From my experience, children begin to want to sleep, as opposed to being the first one up, at around eight years of age. On the eighth birthday, each child is given his own alarm clock. He must set it at night and be up at the specified time.

Take Pan, Will Color

I use Capbe pans with the sliding top for storing children's crayons, pencils, paper, and coloring books. After getting out items, the children have a flat surface to work on. The flat top facilitates storage. Also, the kits are "spill proof" for traveling.

Make the Most of It

When a child is ill and has to stay in bed, use this opportunity to deep-clean in his room. He loves the attention, and you can sort and throw away with his approval and input.

Transport Tube

The inside tubes from waxed paper and aluminum foil make excellent containers for carrying important papers to and from school. They are also good for storing children's drawings.

Color Code

Each of our children has a brightly colored backpack for school. Each one has a specified coat closet hook, color-coded to his pack.

Chief Inspector

Each week we assign a new "chief inspector" to oversee the family chores. He reports in family council meeting on the quality of the work, complaints, and praise. He has a "first mate" who is responsible for seeing that the chores are done. They must meet the inspector's expectations or be done again. Even the smaller children take their turns, assisted by Mother.

New Beginning
One week before school starts, we begin the nightly schedule of baths and new bedtimes. This way the children will be accustomed to it before the actual day arrives.

Two at a Time
When my boys are assigned to work as a team, they seem to enjoy their jobs much more than when they are alone. I encourage them to help each other make their beds, clean the windows, or mop the floors.

A Time to Share
I always hated to be sent to the kitchen by myself. Parents and children can utilize chore time to draw closer to each other. Doing the dishes together can be a time to talk, laugh, teach, and share.

You Do It
I always had difficulty training my children to unfold and turn dirty clothes right side out before putting them into the hamper. I solved the problem by just washing and folding the clothes the way they were, so that the person had to spend his own time and energy turning them right side out when he wanted to wear them.

Points for Departure
In my desperation to teach my children responsibility, I came up with the following plan. I had them brainstorm to determine what activities they might like to do with me at the end of the summer. Everything from going to Disneyland

to visiting the zoo was included on the list. I then attached points to each activity; for instance, going to Disneyland might be fifty points, while going to the zoo would be ten.

The children looked over the list and agreed upon the one thing they wanted most to do. Then they set about earning the necessary points during the summer months. They would get so many points for brushing teeth, putting clothes away, helping mother set the table, and so forth. They would, however, lose points for such things as arguing, whining, and any other negative behavior. They could earn bonus points by doing extra good deeds. I remained in control of issuing points, so that the chart served me and not the other way around. The summer turned out to be quite pleasant, and we had a good time at Disneyland.

It Will Remain There

My son started dumping his clothes all over his bedroom. I found them on his dresser, in the closet, and on the floor. I let them remain where he dropped them until he asked for clean clothes. Then I said, "Look, there's the hamper. Everything in it will be washed, folded, and taken care of by me. Anything left outside of it—well, I guess it'll just remain wherever it is." It worked! I held firm, and he complied.

Study Time

Study time at our home is from 7:00 to 8:00 in the evening. Everyone cooperates. This is the quiet hour, when children observe the whole family reading or working on school projects.

Forewarned

I set the timer for twenty minutes before the children's actual bedtime. This gives them a specific warning that it's time to finish chores, brush teeth, and get ready for bed.

"Hop-to"
We have daily inspection time: 7:30 A.M. on weekdays and 11:00 A.M. on Saturdays. If I find someone's work unfinished, I don't nag, nor will I ever do it for the child. He simply suffers the logical consequence, which is missing breakfast or being late for school on weekdays, and missing out on scheduled activities on Saturday.

Joker Card
Along with the regular chores on our "pocket" chore chart, I include several fun cards. One day a child may find, along with his regular duty cards, a card saying, "Good for one free ice cream cone," or "I'll do the bathroom today."

Morning Preview
Each morning I spend a few moments with my children going over our schedules so they know of any unusual plans. I check with the teenagers for anything I should be aware of in their activities. When it comes to the smaller children, I run through their day and tell them of fun things to look forward to. This provides great incentive for them to hurry through the chores.

Tooth-brushing Timer
To make tooth-brushing time less frantic for my three children, I use my three-minute egg timer. The child sets the timer as he begins. As soon as the timer rings, he must put away the toothpaste and brush and dry the water spots from the sink with a towel, so the next child can come into a clean bathroom.

Star Bonus

My children have a star chart. They get one star each day for completing the day's chores in a satisfactory manner. They also receive extra stars for such things as helping willingly or showing kindness to brothers and sisters. When a child has accumulated twenty stars, he can think of something special he wants to do.

No Room for Doubt

I've found it necessary to be very specific about what I mean when I ask, "Is your room clean?" This is the check-off chart I have in each child's room:

1. Bed made—bottom sheet pulled up smoothly, sides tucked in, no wrinkles.
2. Drawers closed—no clothes hanging out.
3. Clothes picked up and put away—not on bed or on closet floor.
4. Toys—everything—picked up and in its own place.
5. Nightstand and dresser top orderly.
6. Lights out!

Eye Level

Mirror tiles placed at the child's eye level encourage good grooming.

Helpful Sayings

"Some folks are like blisters. They show up when the work is done." (Braude.)

"The hardest work is that which should have been done yesterday." (Braude.)

"It's the biggest mistake to think you are working for someone else." (Cavalier.)

"Work is love made visible." (Gibran.)

WISE USE OF TIME

The "ABC's" of Planning Time

Most time-management experts use some type of "Things-to-Do" list. Making an effective list entails at least one step more than simply jotting down things to be done. After listing everything you'd like to do:

1. Decide which activities you choose to perform today, the "A" priorities. Then determine the order in which you perform them—A-1, A-2, A-3, and so on.

2. Decide which activities you will leave until tomorrow, the "B" priorities. They are important because you *will* perform them, but not today.

3. Decide which activities are unimportant, the "C" priorities. Cross them off your list.

Although a blank sheet of paper will suffice, I have found it helpful to develop a rough planning form that I photocopy in bulk and use on a daily basis. Rather than use someone else's form, it is best to create a form for your own needs. I began with my husband's format but made changes for my own purposes. Therefore, I am not suggesting that the reader should use my format, but it may be helpful as a guide. (See page 141.)

Here are some additional ideas on the "Things-to-Do" list:

1. Be consistent with your choice of paper for making your daily list. If you don't make up your own format to be photocopied, consider using a loose-leaf binder or file cards.

DAY ______ DATE ______ ______ DINNER FOR TONIGHT

GOALS: Today ______

This Month ______

Long Term ______

Today's Schedule:

	A, B or C	To Be Prioritized
6:00		
6:30	○	
7:00	○	
7:15	○	
7:30	○	
7:45	○	
8:00	○	
8:15	○	
8:30	○	
8:45	○	
9:00	○	
9:15	○	
9:30	○	
9:45	○	
10:00	○	
10:15	○	
10:30	○	
10:45	○	
11:00	○	
11:15	○	
11:30	○	
11:45	○	
12:00		
12:15		
12:30		
12:45		
1:00		
1:15		
1:30		
1:45		
2:00		
2:15		
2:30		
2:45		
3:00		
3:15		
3:30		
3:45		
4:00		
4:15		
4:30		
4:45		
5:00		
5:15		
5:30		
5:45		
6:00		
6:15		
6:30		
6:45		
7:00		
7:15		
7:30		
7:45		
8:00		

2. Write your list in pencil, since it will undoubtedly be necessary for you to revise the time schedule from time to time.

3. Add up the time required to accomplish your "A" priorities. This is the total amount of time necessary to accomplish everything that you *must* do during the period of time you are scheduling. Consider also adding time for interruptions.

4. Keep your list available and within easy reach at all times.

5. Do the thing that matters most ("A" priority) first.

6. Do only one thing at a time.

7. Although you see today's calendar on a daily basis, it is also necessary to keep a monthly and weekly appointment and planning calendar.

8. Plan each day, each hour, as though you were paying for it. You are. Your time is your life!

Setting Goals

Each day, before scheduling my day, I write out the current goals I have set for myself. I break them down in five basic categories:

1. Long-range goals (what I want to accomplish or experience before the end of my lifetime.)
2. Five-year goals.
3. One-year goals.
4. Six-month goals.
5. Daily goals.

I prepare my list daily, giving each goal a realistic target date. Sometimes this seems repetitive, but I feel that we get what we *expect* to get in this life. I try to include one thing—small or large—on my daily list that will bring me closer to my long-range goals.

Procrastination

I have found that when I put off doing what I know really should be done, I end up being more drained than if I'd done the job twice. You can't sit back and wait for the energy—sometimes it doesn't come until the project is nearly finished.

No More a Martyr

For fifteen years, I felt guilty about spending time for myself. I had to be so ill that I could barely move before I'd justify not keeping everything immaculate. I had to be exhausted and close to a nervous breakdown before I'd get a babysitter and get out of the house for an afternoon alone. I think I felt that being a martyr was synonymous with being unselfish. Since then, I have learned that by spending the needed time on myself, I carry less resentments and have even more to give, in terms of time, than ever before.

Good Haircut Saves Time

This may seem frivolous, but a good haircut to me is an absolute necessity. My time is valuable, and having my hair trimmed regularly saves hours and hours of fussing and keeps my self-esteem intact.

Saying "No" Gracefully

Realizing that my time simply won't permit my saying yes to everything, I have found the following to be helpful in assigning priorities to situations:

1. Is it something I want to do?
2. Will my family suffer (in terms of time and attention) if I accept?
3. Will my main Church calling suffer if I accept?

4. Will my husband and family support my use of time here?

If I find that my family's needs require a "no" answer, I don't make excuses, nor do I defend my situation. I say, "I'm so flattered that you'd think of asking me, but I won't be able to join you this time. Thank you for thinking of me."

This exercise helps me to feel less guilty about not being able to be all things to all people. It has also helped me see that I am the only one who is responsible and to blame if my energy isn't put where it's needed most.

Message Center

A message center can be a real time-saver for the family. A large bulletin board might serve your purpose, or you can custom-design a center with cork tiles or roll-out cork. Consider the following:

—Lots of push tacks
—Large calendar with big squares
—Hanging pencil
—Paper holder
—Chore chart

Time Wasters

When I realized I was interrupted so often that I wasn't finishing my scheduled work, I itemized all interruptions during the course of two days. Then I could see the pattern and could figure out ways to eliminate interruptions.

One of the first things I had to do was to end the open-door policy I had with my children. I had to let them know that I would not be available at certain times. They just would have to respect my scripture-reading and concentrating moments. I also could see that there were certain interruptions I could eliminate by anticipating them beforehand. The "I'm-hungry" requests could be solved simply by having a plate of vegetables prepared and available to be eaten at random.

Call Backs

When the phone rings on a busy day, I respond with "I have an appointment right now. May I call you back at 3:30?" I schedule all phone calls to be returned at that hour. I limit the total amount of call-back time to half an hour.

Not Available

Periodically, I will take the phone off the hook. When I do this, I always let my husband know, so that in an emergency I can be reached through a neighbor.

"Time"

Make a "Time" sign and hang it on the phone to remind you of the time you are spending.

Hourglass Honesty

I keep a three-minute timer by the phone, and try to get all necessary information out of the way within that amount of time. This is also great for long distance calls—you know when your three minutes are up.

Meal-Planning Cards

By making my own personalized meal-planning cards, I have saved literally hundreds of hours each year. They help me serve interesting, well-planned meals with variety, economy, and very little work. It takes a little time in the beginning to make the cards, but once you have them, the work is done and they will really work for you. Here's how I do it:

Take one day to go through all of your recipe files and make a "master list" of all of your favorite, tried-and-true recipes. You'll be surprised how many different meals you do cook!

On file cards, separate the dishes by recipe name and page number. Make one card for each of the following:

1. Main dishes
    - A. Hamburger dishes
    - B. Chicken
    - C. Beef
    - D. Meatless (soup, cheese, egg)
    - E. Miscellaneous (pork, turkey, seafood)
2. Vegetables
3. Salads (include interesting dressings)
4. Desserts

Now, take clean cards and begin planning weekly menus. Break each card down into seven days. Go to the master lists and choose seven main dishes. Include at least one chicken, one hamburger, one beef, and several meatless dishes. Choose vegetables, salads, and desserts that add complementary texture, color, and variety to each main dish.

You'll be surprised how many different menus you will come up with. When I finished, I had ten weekly cards, which I covered with clear plastic. I continue to add to both the master lists and the collection of meal-planning cards. I rotate the cards, and on my grocery shopping day, the card I will use serves as the basis for my weekly shopping list.

Time Saving

When I make my menus for the month, I write down twenty-five main dishes, substituting leftovers for the remaining days. Then, throughout the month, I mark each dish off as I prepare it. This works best for me because on some days I don't feel like making what I had planned.

Time for Each Other

If a relationship is to flourish and grow, it needs time and caring. We need time for nurturing what we already have, time for knowing each other better, and time for sharing. We can't afford to let the good times merely happen; we must make time for each other. The following are some helpful ideas:

1. At least once or twice a year get away for a weekend. Take calendars, set goals, and have a planning session together. This doesn't have to be elaborate—many couples say they periodically get away for a night or two right in their own home town.
2. Make it a rule that when you're alone together in your room, no one may enter.
3. Take the phone off the hook when you're talking.
4. Go for a drive, and park to discuss important subjects. Sometimes solitude is priceless!
5. Meet for lunch.
6. Go to the library, where it's quiet.
7. Make date night sacred! Get a standing babysitter, if your children are small. This will keep you from making excuses.
8. Set aside one morning for sleeping in.
9. Jog together in the early morning or evening.
10. Read a book together.
11. Schedule a time, such as the day after family home evening to discuss children and plans. Sometimes this has to begin with a formal appointment time, but you may enjoy it enough that later you won't need an appointment.

12. When the phone rings and you're together, have the children ask if you may return the call.
13. Take a walk regularly.
14. Share a mutual hobby.
15. Buy season tickets for the theater or symphony.
16. Visit a museum.

NINETY TIME-SAVING IDEAS

Planning Your Time

1. Write down your goals every day—long-term and present.

2. Become a yearly and monthly planner. That's the way your dreams materialize.

3. Develop your stamina for staying with a task for an extended period of time.

4. Break difficult tasks down into smaller portions. Hack away at a job in pieces until it's finished.

5. Be aware of experts who are available to help you. Find ways for making these services available.

6. Find something positive in each situation.

7. Eliminate as many interruptions as possible.

8. Allow some "do-nothing" time. Use it to be creative and to generate new ideas.

9. Buy the biggest possible calendar to plan monthly activities with your family.

10. Respect starting times. If you are conducting a meeting and only you and one other person are present at the given hour, start anyway. Time is life, and life is precious.

11. Handle things only once. Put them where they belong the first time.

12. Get up early!

13. Be aware of how each success has a tendency to build.

14. When you plan time for yourself, don't let anything, save a dire emergency, interrupt it.

15. Be aware of anything that might be delegated to someone else. Also, be aware of your resistances to delegating, and work on them.

16. Don't do anything that should be done by someone else.

17. Arrange your day so that your most important work is done at *your* prime time.

18. Try to do one job completely and only once. Divide your chores into imaginary sections; then finish one section at a time. This way you avoid repeating or overlooking some jobs.

19. Set a time limit on any project you undertake. Allow yourself to feel the contentment of a job well done. Sometimes the hardest and yet most necessary task is realizing when to quit and relax.

20. Carry lesson books with you to take advantage of waiting time.

21. Don't get behind. It takes much less time to keep up than to catch up.

22. Write down appointments as soon as you make them.

23. Enjoy whatever it is that you're doing. If it's so unpleasant that you can't enjoy it, reevaluate your schedule.

Around the House

24. Keep your clock at least five minutes fast.

25. Monitor television watching closely.

26. Don't eat a heavy lunch. It lowers your effectiveness.

27. Don't apologize if someone comes unexpectedly to your door. Your time is spent on your priorities, not theirs.

28. Keep a separate file folder for each member of the family.

29. When you bring home library books, write on your calendar the due dates at least four or five days in advance of the actual day the books are to be returned.

30. Keep a tape recorder handy and ready to use.

31. Exercise. You have more energy when you're physically fit.

32. Plan all dental and routine doctor appointments for summer months.

33. Pretend someone is coming at 4:00 P.M. (or another arbitrary hour), so the housework will be done by that time.

34. Create a place in your home for hobbies. Find ways to keep it organized and confined to a particular area.

35. Have one container, such as a box or drawer, for paper, pens, envelopes, and stamps.

36. Buy long cords for all phones.

37. Tape the master key for bathrooms to the door casing, so it can be found quickly.

Shopping

38. Shop at off-peak hours. You can save time in check-out lines, and the selection of produce is often better.

39. Shop once a week or even once a month.

40. Take advantage of stores with late hours. A busy mother or father can shop in the evening, without dragging children along or feeling rushed.

41. Do Christmas shopping all year round. Take advantage of sales. Keep an ongoing list of who needs what.

42. Avoid last-minute rushes by having a gift shelf at home stocked with suitable gifts for all occasions.

43. Keep a calendar with dates to be remembered, and shop for greeting cards all at once. Keep them in a special file.

44. Shop by phone.
45. Shop by catalog.
46. Tear your grocery list into sections and give your child or children a certain amount of time to gather the listed items and be back at the check-out counter.
47. Group your shopping by store location.

In the Kitchen

48. Keep a supply of paper cups and plates handy to save clean-up time in emergency situations.
49. Find a store or restaurant supply house that sells colorful paper placemats. They save a large family a great deal of time. Keep a wide variety on hand, including some with games, maps, or wise sayings to spark dinner-table conversation.
50. Keep the ingredients for a favorite, easily prepared meal tucked away and ready for unexpected guests.
51. For times when unexpected company arrives and the cupboards are bare, have a list handy of good, inexpensive take-out restaurants.
52. Use your freezer. Make double portions of each meal and freeze leftovers.
53. On less hectic days, make and freeze pancakes and waffles. On busy days, simply pop them into the toaster.
54. Make sandwiches ahead and store them in the freezer. Most are good for at least two weeks. On Saturday, make and freeze sandwiches for the week. Use peanut butter, cold cuts, chicken, turkey, cheese, and tuna. Mayonnaise can be used if its volume doesn't exceed one-third of the total sandwich. Butter both sides of bread to prevent sogginess.
55. Put aluminum foil under stove burners and in the refrigerator for quick cleanup of spills.

56. Clean a badly burned pan by soaking it in boiling water and baking soda. You can also add fabric softener to the water. Within an hour the pan will be ready to clean.

57. To hasten clean-up time when bread dough is stuck to the bread board, sprinkle it well with salt and rub with a dishcloth.

58. Hang a mirror near the kitchen sink for quick grooming.

Housework Time Savers

59. Use dishwashing crystals to remove heavy bathtub ring.

60. Sprinkle cleaner in the bath water before draining it, and there will be no ring to clean.

61. Tie a plastic garbage bag to the handle of your upright vacuum cleaner, and pick up clutter as you vacuum.

62. Hose down the front porch instead of sweeping it.

63. Keep cleaning supplies, including paper towels for cleaning the mirror, in each bathroom.

64. Keep a dust cloth tucked away in each room, or invest in a nice feather duster.

65. To keep the mop from becoming stiff, add a small amount of fabric softener to the last rinse water before putting it away.

66. Cover minor scratches in furniture with a compatible color of shoe polish or crayon.

67. To empty the toilet bowl for a thorough cleaning, dump a pail of water into the bowl, and it will empty out.

68. Store plastic trash liners in the garbage can. As you fill one, simply lift it out, and a new liner will be ready for use.

69. Hang a decorative drawstring bag at the top and bottom of the stairs. It's great for storing items away until the next trip up or down.

70. Hair spray or rubbing alcohol will remove purple price-tag marks from plastic products or counter tops.

71. Keep a "home-improvement book" for easy reference. Include color names and samples of wall coverings, paint, and drapes, as well as information on all appliances and home improvements.

Children Time Savers

72. Install a drinking fountain outdoors.

73. Teach children how to get a drink of water in a paper cup from the tap in the bathtub.

74. Keep a drawerful of bright bandanas for children's bibs. (This isn't as intimidating for older children.)

75. Set out all your children's clothes for the next day when they go to bed. Include hair needs as well.

76. Spray baby's white shoes with hair spray for a longer-lasting polish. This also helps keep polish from rubbing onto other clothes.

77. Punch three holes in children's artwork, and keep it in a looseleaf binder. This saves time and space.

78. Take the phone off the hook while bathing children.

79. Hang a towel over the top of the bathroom door when children are in the bathroom alone, so they won't accidentally (or otherwise) lock themselves in.

80. Next time you redecorate, consider buying colorful comforters for the children's beds. They serve as both blanket and bedspread. They wash beautifully, and the beds are much easier to make than when you use traditional bedding.

81. Let your child "hire" you to clean his room, if it isn't done by a certain time.

82. "Hire" your child to do extra household chores to help lighten your load.

Clothing and Laundry

83. Get rid of clothes you and the children don't wear. The fewer clothes you have, the fewer there are to care for.

84. Mix and match your clothing. Carefully color-coordinate everything—for the children as well as yourself. Fewer clothes properly selected and coordinated are worth more than a closet or drawer full of odds and ends.

85. To save laundry time on the sheets of very small children, turn them head to foot. The children only dirty half of the sheet at a time.

86. To keep the nap of velvet looking good, press a velvet garment right side down on a thick terrycloth towel. Press with warm iron on wrong side of fabric.

87. Add a cupful of vinegar to the last rinse cycle of the wash to minimize lint from dark clothing.

And finally . . .

88. Don't get behind. It takes much less time to keep up than to catch up.

89. Forget the failures of yesterday. Today is a new beginning.

90. Ask yourself continually, "What is the best use of my time right now?" Sometimes this changes drastically from what you had expected. The important thing is that each minute be filled with the things that matter most to you!

5

LIVING WITHIN YOUR MEANS

Ye Latter-day Saints,
learn to sustain yourselves,
produce everything you need to eat,
drink or wear;
and if you cannot obtain
all you wish for today,
learn to do without that
which you cannot purchase and pay for;
and bring your minds into subjection
that you must and will live
within your means.
(Brigham Young, Journal of Discourses *12:231.)*

AN ATTITUDE

Worth More Than Money

As an exercise in determining our family's priorities, we take time at one family home evening every year to make a list of at least eight things we currently value more than money. After sharing them, we record them in our journals.

Not Ours to Spend

My husband and I have found that giving money to the Lord blesses us more than we know. We don't ever consider ten percent of our money as "ours." In this way, we avoid resentment or feelings that "if we only had that money, we could . . ."

Appreciation for Luxuries

The following are some ideas a family can use to teach appreciation for the luxuries they have:

1. Live for at least a week on the amount of money a welfare recipient would have.
2. Turn off the heat in your home for two days.
3. Take ten dollars to a Goodwill or Deseret Industries store and see how far it will go. Could it buy a dress? a shirt?

4. Give each child two dollars and send him into the grocery store to buy a portion of a dinner, such as the vegetable, a salad, or dessert.

5. Take a ride into a ghetto, or visit an unemployment office and just watch.

A FAMILY AFFAIR

Money-Saving Ideas

When I knew we needed to be on a strict budget, I asked everyone in the family to write down ten ways in which he or she could save money. They then had to order their list from one to ten, number ten being the most difficult to give up. When we compared lists, we found that we agreed on many things. Also, some family members thought of unique ways to save that might have otherwise not been acknowledged. For instance, one of my children suggested that we give birthday gifts to other children by selecting toys in good condition from his toy box. No one had to give up anything rated as number six through ten unless he so desired.

Determining Priorities

My wife and I determine priorities by brainstorming how each of us would spend $500,000. This helps us establish long-range goals in terms of what we value most and where we want to be ten years from now. After comparing lists and discussing future goals, we reduce the amount to $50,000. We each make our own list, assigning priorities to our purchases. We again compare notes, working together with our budget book until we have narrowed the list down to one or two items—a vacation, a new car— which then become the financial goals for this year.

Involve the Whole Family

Involving the whole family in budgeting has many benefits. It gives the children an opportunity to be apprentices at learning to manage money. It helps them feel a part of the decision-making process. It also reduces friction and resentments.

A Money Book

When we knew we had to budget our money, we wanted everyone in the family to feel the need for working as a unit, so we asked everyone to keep track of his expenditures, no matter how small. We gave each child a money book in which he recorded what he spent. At the end of the month, we pooled our books in order to see the habits we had formed, both individually and as a family. It was easy to see what we could give up, and each family member promised to eliminate certain specific expenditures. Each made his own decision, so that no one felt imposed upon.

How Will You Pay for It?

When a child wants something that is not within your (or his) budget, let him tell you how he plans to pay for it. Don't be afraid to let him work and save for it.

Dream Folder

Our family keeps a "dream folder." We collect pictures and brochures of the items we dream about owning someday. Periodically, when we have a little money saved, we will take the folder out and select the item that currently takes priority. This year it is a piano, so that our oldest child can begin taking lessons. We feel that this is a good way to teach the children to set goals. They also learn that dreams really can come true.

Allowance for Mom and Dad

No matter how tight the money situation is in our home, my husband and I have found it absolutely necessary to provide some kind of personal allowance for each of us. This gives us a degree of freedom and lessens tension.

Catch-All Jar

We keep a jar on the kitchen counter into which we place all grocery receipts. At the end of the month, we total up the receipts to get an accurate account of what we are spending at the grocery store. Sometimes we will allow one of the children to be the family bookkeeper. He will be responsible for totaling the receipts and reporting the amount to the family.

Money Management Center

We have one specific place (a desk in the family room) where we handle all of our family money matters. We all know that this is where "business" takes place. We keep it neat and tidy so that we can always find what we're looking for. Keeping the clutter away is incentive for keeping up with family business. Here are some of the items we keep within easy reach:

—Bills ("to be paid" and "paid").

—All family records.

—One jar for grocery receipts and a separate jar for all other receipts. (At the end of each month, we file these in envelopes labeled with the corresponding month.)

—Money record book.

—Calendar.
—Stationery.
—Checkbooks.
—Cancelled checks.
—Pens and pencils.
—Stamps.
—Rubber bands.
—Scissors.
—Scotch tape.
—Stapler.

A Joint Effort

We make it a family affair to check the newspaper for the weekly food bargains. One person looks for best meat buys, one for best fruit and vegetable buys, one for toiletries, and so on. At the end of our search, we compare our findings for the best buys and make up the weekly shopping list, including one food-storage purchase each week.

What Are My Habits?

No one can change his habits without understanding what those habits are. I was surprised to see my spending patterns when I asked myself these questions. How did I spend—

1. the money I received for my birthday? Christmas?
2. the change in my wallet? in the piggy bank?
3. the fifty dollars I dreamed I found?
4. my money for entertainment last weekend? the weekend before?
5. my lunch money?
6. my last twenty dollars of "spending money"?

TEACHING CHILDREN THE VALUE OF MONEY

Forming a Habit
We have found that it is wise to teach children to pay tithing and save for missions as soon as they are old enough to hold money in their little hands. Walking to the bishop's office with a tithing envelope is an uplifting, responsible experience for little ones, even if the contribution is only a penny. We opened a mission account in the bank for each of our children at birth. We add to the accounts on each birthday and expect the children to add a certain percentage of their allowance each time they receive it. If they can develop this habit when young, it will continue throughout life.

Tithing Settlement
It has been an uplifting experience for our entire family to attend tithing settlement once a year with the bishop. We make it a policy to attend those meetings regularly.

Ten Percent Policy
When our children receive money, we have a rule that they pay ten percent to the Lord. The balance is then split between savings and spending money. Note: A teenager may feel his free agency is curtailed unless this policy is started at a very young age.

Dollar for Dollar

We match dollar for dollar any money our son deposits into his mission account.

Money Needs vs. Wants

Children need to distinguish between what they *need* and what they *want*. We asked our children to list fifteen items they would like to own. They had an entire week to think and plan out their lists. They could cut pictures from ads and make a wish book, if they chose. The next week, lists ready, they were to write "N" next to the items they really needed and "W" next to those they just wanted. Then they were to put a double star next to the item they wanted most of all. We discussed the difference between want and need, and brainstormed ways in which they could earn the money to get what they wanted most of all.

Planning a Party

Periodically, I let the older children (eight and up) plan a little party or luncheon for which they are totally responsible, including planning the menu and purchasing all necessary items. I give them a base figure, $5.00 or so, and they must keep all purchases within that amount.

Expectations of Teens

We expect our teenagers to pay their own telephone expenses, to be able to pay for car insurance before getting a driver's license, and to pay for all gas used in the family car.

Birthday Choice

I give my children a choice between having a birthday party or getting a present from Mom and Dad. Parties cost a great deal—as do gifts—so we find this policy helpful for a tight budget. Giving them free agency helps them to appreciate the decision they make.

Little Ones Can Help

While shopping, give the children your "cents-off" coupons and have them find the corresponding items.

Matching Funds

To make saving money more enticing for the children, my husband and I have a firm, standing offer to match any money they are able to save and deposit into their own bank accounts.

No Vacation Nagging

We meet with our children to plan our vacations. We buy a notebook and let them plan and be in charge of how we will spend our predetermined amount of vacation money.

Comparison Shopping

We teach our older children to understand and take advantage of unit pricing. We may say, "Even though the giant-size jar of mayonnaise is cheaper per ounce, it isn't the best buy for us because of the shelf life compared to our family size."

At the Check-out Line

When my child is with me in the grocery store, I will give him a certain amount of money and let him buy the oranges and apples, the cereal, or some such item. It takes longer in line, and sometimes those waiting behind me don't appreciate the added time, but I want my children to learn from an early age the association between money and goods.

How Would You Spend It?

On Wednesday evening as I go through grocery ads in the paper, I include the children. I give them an imaginary amount of money and a piece of paper and pencil. John decides how he will spend ten dollars. Elizabeth decides how she will spend twenty dollars. Krissy, my sixteen-year-old, can decide how she would spend the whole week's grocery money. Sometimes her list is good enough that I let her do the shopping with very few revisions.

Commercials Are Traps

Sometimes my children become enthralled with a particular product that is grossly overrated on TV. I will spend time at the store with them looking at such an item, showing and explaining how it doesn't measure up to what the man on TV claimed about it.

Coin Collections

One person who helped my children save money was their grandmother, who gave them an interest in coin collecting. One child would save dimes as a specialty, while another would save quarters, or silver coins.

ALLOWANCES

Is It for Us?

Many parents prefer to run their homes on a money-as-needed basis. This works very well for some homes, and there are many good ideas for making that system work. However, most child development experts and many parents still feel that giving the child an allowance provides the means for him to learn many things about controlling himself and about life. Some of the potential lessons might be: cause and effect as he makes mistakes in judgment, effective decision-making, responsibility.

Allowance How-to's

While there is no set formula for success, those who make an allowance a meaningful experience for their children and themselves agree on several basic points. Fundamental questions that must be answered in the affirmative by the parent are:

1. Am I willing to be consistent?
2. Am I willing to give him the agreed-upon amount on the given day every single week?
3. Do I have the discipline (or can I muster it)
4. Can I let the child make mistakes without criticizing him?

5. When he fumbles and makes mistakes, am I willing to let him suffer the logical consequences, which might be going without?

6. Can I resist coming to the rescue?

Before presenting the idea of allowance to your child, consider the following suggestions:

1. Make a list of the exact items for which he will be responsible.

2. Determine a reasonable amount for covering those expenses. (If the figure seems large, consider the amount that you spend each week on these things and ask yourself if you are willing to let him assume responsibility for paying for them. If not, modify the amount and continue to be specific.)

3. Decide whether or not there will be exceptions, such as large purchases or an unexpected invitation somewhere.

4. Make a list of activities and purchases that are not in keeping with family rules and are not acceptable despite the fact that it's "his" money.

5. When you come up with the figure and exactly what it will cover, be sure you have allowed the child a certain amount to play with. With this amount, he will learn to make decisions on his own.

6. Be willing to keep close contact with the child and how he is handling his allowance for the first few weeks. Be prepared to assess and reassess with him until you know that what you've planned is workable.

7. When you've decided to go ahead, discuss thoroughly with your child all of these steps, making sure there are no misunderstandings.

A Privilege

In our home, having an allowance is a privilege. It is not tied to housework, which is a child's responsibility as a family member. However, we do require that all assigned jobs be completed within a given period of time. When a child fails to follow through, I pay someone else to do the job and deduct the cost from his allowance. I say, "You may choose not to do it, but guess who will pay for having it done?"

Words to the Rescue

Saturday is allowance day at our home. Each child receives enough to provide some recreational activities for himself. It's hard when the children say over and over, "Please, may I have this?" I have two pet phrases that I memorize and force myself to use:

1. "Sure, you may have it. Use your allowance."
2. "I'll see you on Saturday."

Eventually they do learn to make their money stretch—maybe not for everything, but for what they *really* want.

Break It Down

When we decided to give our fifteen-year-old son an allowance, we agreed upon a monthly figure that would include everything, including clothes. The monthly figure was more than we felt he could budget, with his limited experience, so at the beginning of each month, we'd divide the money into four envelopes and tack one envelope to his bulletin board every Friday. After two months, we'd put two envelopes up at a time. Eventually he became secure enough in his planning and budgeting that we were able to give him the monthly figure in a lump sum.

Extra Opportunity

We give the children opportunities to earn extra money by doing extra work, beyond their normal household workload.

You Talk—You Pay

If teenagers want their own phone, make a set of rules. The first one is that they pay for it themselves.

SEVENTY-FIVE MONEY-SAVING IDEAS

Food

1. Buy cuts of meat, such as round steak, in bulk. If you have a family of six, buy six whole steaks. Find out from the butcher which sections are tender and which need longer cooking. Divide each steak into individual sections, and you will have twelve minute steaks, twelve Swiss steaks, and stew meat.

2. Look for the cuts of meat that give the best value in actual meat per pound. For instance, I find that chicken breasts costing $1.39 per pound give our family more meat than whole fryers at 79¢ per pound. Many beef cuts are the same.

3. Buy large cuts of meat and cut them up yourself.

4. Grow as much of your own food as possible.

5. Buy generic brands. Try them first, however, to make sure your family approves of the quality of each item. I have found the paper products and plastic garbage bags to be good.

6. By eliminating cold cereals, we save a great deal of money. I make homemade granola or use easily prepared oatmeal and Cream of Wheat.

8. Buy a wok! Learn to prepare and enjoy inexpensive Chinese foods and stir-fry vegetables. (You use very little meat.)

9. Buy cheese in bulk. Set aside what you will use within a reasonable amount of time and grate the rest. Freeze in plastic bags. This has been a great time and money saver for us because we eat less cheese for snacking, and the grated cheese is always ready to use in recipes.

10. Grated potatoes are a good extender for meatloaf or hamburgers. Also try using them to thicken stews.

11. Put leftover vegetables in a container in the refrigerator, to be used later for homemade vegetable soup.

12. Adding a good bouillon base to homemade soup helps you use less meat and will turn a weak stock into hearty soup.

13. Serve homemade soup, warm bread, and salad once a week for dinner.

14. Take the time to write out your weekly minutes. Save them from week to week, covered with plastic for easy reference.

15. If you cover moldy cheese in a container with a few sugar lumps, the mold will disappear.

16. Wilted lettuce can be revived by putting it first in hot water, then in ice water with added vinegar or lemon.

17. Overripe bananas can be mashed and frozen for making banana bread at a later date. Also, try freezing them to make nutritious Popsicles.

18. Egg whites can be frozen and stored for up to one year.

19. Add a little cornstarch mixed with cold water to homemade maple syrup. You can use less sugar and still have a thick, rich syrup.

20. Remember that you pay for the small, pretty package. Buy things like raisins in larger quantities and break them down into plastic bags yourself.

21. Examine convenience foods with a critical eye. Some save very little work and are quite expensive. Others, such as frozen french fries, orange juice, and fish, are work and money savers and are therefore bargains.

22. Use a dehydrator to preserve fruits and vegetables in season. You can also take advantage of lower prices on overripe fruit year round. Ripe fruit is perfect for dehydrating.

23. Keeping popcorn in the freezer makes the popcorn fresher and helps eliminate "old maids."

24. Look for day-old bread and pastries in the grocery store, bakery, or bakery outlet.

25. When shopping, take a calculator with you.

26. Buy bread by weight, not size. Some large loaves are really just filled with air.

27. Small eggs are cheaper per pound than large ones.

28. Shop for advertised specials.

29. Buy by the case.

30. Read labels carefully. Direct your money at the food that gives the most nutrition per dollar.

31. When shopping for groceries:

a. Leave very young children at home.

b. Don't go when you're hungry.

c. Take a list.

d. Stick to the list, praying for self-control.

32. Surveys reveal that the shopper who stays longer than thirty minutes in the grocery store spends an average of fifty cents a minute!

Become a Conscious—and Conscientious—Consumer

33. Resolve to return inferior merchandise and demand better quality. That is the only way the consumer will win.

34. Keep in one place all receipts for purchases other than groceries, in case you need to return an item to the store.

35. Whenever you make a purchase of any kind, check with the store about the return policy.

36. If you make a spur-of-the-moment decision to buy from a door-to-door salesman and sign your name to a contract, you usually have three days to cancel the deal, should you change your mind. You must notify the company, in writing, that you want to cancel the deal you've just signed. Make and keep a copy of your letter. Check with your state consumer affairs department to determine local regulations concerning cancellation of such contracts.

37. Don't take more money with you than you'll realistically need when you go shopping.

38. Destroy your credit cards if the accounts are not being paid monthly or if you are making purchases you wouldn't make with cash.

39. Think of each purchase in terms of a trade-off: "What will I give up later in order to have what I want so badly right now?"

40. Check with your doctor to see if you can purchase generic-brand prescriptions. Call ahead to different pharmacies and do some comparison shopping. You'll be surprised at the price range for the same drug.

Around the House

41. Store batteries in the refrigerator. They will last longer.

42. Used greeting cards, trimmed a little, make lovely gift tags.

43. Iron used gift-wrapping paper; it will be almost like new.

44. A piece of charcoal slipped into Dad's tool box will help prevent rust.

45. Sharpen dull scissors by cutting sandpaper with them.

46. Clean rust and film from bathroom fixtures with kerosene.

47. Collect small soap pieces and dissolve them by boiling. This makes a solution that can be added to a pump container for washing hands and fine lingerie.

48. Vinegar is an excellent hair rinse for brunettes. Lemon juice is good for blondes.

49. A good ceramic tile cleaner can be made by mixing equal parts of baking soda and bleach.

50. Need a good window-cleaning or glass shower door solution? Add two tablespoons white vinegar and six tablespoons ammonia to two cups water. Fill an empty spray bottle and clean away!

51. For homemade wax remover, mix one part ammonia with ten parts water. Let the mixture stand ten minutes; then use with a scouring pad to scrub wax off. Be sure to rinse well with clean water.

52. For an inexpensive, all-purpose household cleaner, you might try one of these: (1) mix one tablespoon TSP (trisodium phosphate, available at hardware or paint stores) with one quart water. (2) Add one-half cup ammonia and one-third cup washing soda (sal soda) to a gallon of water.

Clothing and Sewing

53. My husband and I have agreed upon a yearly clothing allowance. I have a special account and receive half of the yearly amount every six months. At first it seemed like a lot of money, but I am actually able to save money by taking advantage of seasonal buying by coordinating my clothing colors.

54. I recently saw a beautiful patchwork afghan made of squares cut from sweaters. I am now collecting our old sweaters and finding others at thrift stores and garage sales, so that I will have enough for a quilt of my own.

55. Take time to make sure any clothing you buy fits well. A sale dress isn't a bargain at any price if you don't wear it.

56. Spend the most money on the clothes you wear the most.

57. To avoid the impulse of the "great buy," remember: it's a bargain only (1) when the price is less than expected, (2) when the item fits well and is of good quality, and (3) when the color is right. Buy only if you have an inner feeling that regardless of the low price, you really like the item and it looks good on you.

58. Holes in knits can be stitched easily with a single thread from the inside of the garment. Catch the loops, and don't pull too tightly. Many larger cities have clothing outlets that sell shirts and dresses with these tiny holes. You can buy these items at low prices and fix them up quickly and easily.

59. I saved all the clothes my children outgrew in what I called my "what-if" barrel. It has come in handy many times. One little boy in our ward who had outgrown his shoes was delighted with a pair my son had worn. My youngest son doesn't realize he's been wearing his older sister's red jacket. Some wards have a clothing exchange where those in need can find treasures in others' outgrown items.

60. Add dishwashing crystals to laundry to whiten and brighten nylon and fine washables.

Share the Expense

61. Share with another family the cost of large items, such as a dehydrator, an apple juicer, or a wheat grinder. Share also on the upkeep.

62. We have formed a mini co-op. We chose several families we felt we could work well with and set up a system where we swap shopping services. We scout out the best buys, and each week one person goes to the fruit market, another to

an egg farm, another to a thrift store for toilet supplies, and so on. Then we meet at a specified location and exchange items.

63. Organize a neighborhood toy and children's clothing swap.

64. Form a babysitting co-op.

65. Form car pools wherever possible.

66. We trade houses for a month with friends in a distant town. This really cuts down on our vacation expenses.

Family Responsibilities

67. Require the children to work for anything that is a frivolous or out-of-the-ordinary expense. Give each chore a price.

68. Stretch recreation money by not eating out on the same night as you go to the movie.

69. Budget by using an envelope system (putting in an envelope the amount for each bill to be paid). This keeps you from thinking you have more money than you really do have.

70. Our family policy is to walk anywhere we are going that is within a mile.

For Free

71. Take advantage of the agricultural extension services in your area. They answer just about any question you have regarding nutrition and canning.

72. Don't forget to take advantage of the public library. Rather than buy that expensive new item, call and ask for a list of what's available in books, records, tapes, and pictures.

73. You can save money by collecting your own free or minimally priced wood from a national forest. Logs, dead

trees, or leftovers from logging ventures are often available. The Forest Service District Ranger's Office, listed in the phone book under "U.S. Government, Department of Agriculture, Forest Service," will tell you where to cut and inform you of the rules and regulations. They may issue you a permit to do your own cutting and hauling.

74. The Consumer Information Center is a service that not too many people use. We pay for it with tax dollars, and it offers us a wide selection of information on almost any topic imaginable. Write for a catalogue of booklets available:

Consumer Information Center
Dept. 50
Pueblo, Colorado 81009

75. Be grateful for every good thing with which the Lord has blessed you.

6

THE SABBATH DAY

And that thou mayest
more fully keep thyself unspotted
from the world,
thou shalt go to the house of prayer
and offer up thy sacraments
upon my holy day;
for verily this is a day
appointed unto you
to rest from your labors,
and to pay thy devotions
unto the Most High.

(D&C 59:9-10.)

A HOLY DAY

Sunday Clothes in Dad's Closet

My husband keeps our son's Sunday clothes, including everything from socks to ties, in his closet. It is his responsibility to get the boys ready for church.

Don't Disturb Me

We set an alarm clock on Sunday for the early risers in our house. They must stay in their rooms until the alarm goes off at eight o'clock. We don't start our family Sunday activities until then, because we need to start the day off in quiet.

Pillow Surprise

"Oh, it's the Sabbath day! I wonder what Dad put under my pillow," Johnny may ask when he wakes up. He may find a juicy orange, a little package of peanuts, or maybe just a note saying, "Johnny, I watched you pick Jane back up when she fell yesterday. I'm proud to have such a thoughtful son!"

Save That for the Sabbath

In order to make the Sabbath joyful, I help my children anticipate it by telling them that we will save that candy until Sunday, or that we'll read that book on Sunday, because it's such a special day. They now sense that Sunday is a happy day to anticipate, not one to dread.

Quiet Time
After church, we have a quiet time in our home, when each person stays in his own room. Before quiet time, we discuss which classical records or hymns will be played. We then put a selection on the record player. When the record is finished, quiet time is over.

Joining Forces
My husband and I set aside every Sunday evening to discuss our children, establish family rules, and jointly solve family problems.

Good Example
When nonmembers ask me to babysit on Sunday, I tell them that I prefer not to work on Sundays, because I enjoy attending church. They sometimes will say, "My, I wish I had a church to go to that I felt that way about." I tell them, "Come to church with me. I'll pick you up."

Strong Temptation
One Sunday our neighbors were having a garage sale. My daughter had gone to it on Saturday when I wasn't home, and she told me they had little miniatures for sale—something I truly enjoy. The temptation to run over just to look welled up inside me so strongly that I almost yielded to it. But I knew that if I did, my example would work against my more

important goal of teaching my daughter to control her impulses enough to obey the Sabbath. I shared my feelings with her: "I really can feel the temptation strongly, but it's more important to me to obey the Sabbath. Sometimes it's difficult to be obedient, but we can be strong."

Did You Go to the Game?

We had been determined to keep the Sabbath day holy when my son played soccer. Normally his games were on other days, but a big playoff game was scheduled for Sunday. It was the most important game of the entire year, but we reminded him of the Sabbath-day rule. With great pain, he missed that game. The next Sunday one of his teammates, who was a member of the Church, asked him why he didn't play. My son was crushed to find out that his friend had been allowed to play in the game. I took this opportunity to teach him about free agency and family rules. "We all have the right to choose what to do, but we don't have the power to choose the results of what we do. Don't condemn him because his family rules are different. We have our rules in our family and he has his. That is the way it is."

General Conference on Television

We found it very difficult to listen to the general conference talks on television because the children were so noisy and restless. We solved the problem by providing them each with a mural-sized sheet of butcher paper and a handful of crayons. We then asked each child to find a place away from the others to work on an art project relating to the topic of the speaker. The rule is that no one can talk during conference, but during family home evening the children can explain and display their artwork. It usually stays on the wall for one week.

Sunday Cook

Dad does the cooking on Sunday, so Mom gets a break. He likes to do it, and the children get some different recipe approaches because he makes up his own!

List of Do's

We have a list of all the things that can be done on Sunday. When someone complains about all the things he can't do, we refer him to the list of the things he *can* do. If a child wants to skate, for example, we tell him that he can do it on Monday or some other day, so that he doesn't feel discouraged.

Prayer Rock

My daughter brought home a little rock from her Primary class. It is painted with a few flowers and has "Prayer Rock" written on it. She places it under her pillow every morning, so that when she puts her head down, the rock will be there to remind her to say her prayers. After she says them, she puts the rock on the floor beside her bed. In the morning, when she steps on it, it will remind her to pray.

Meditation Time

I need quiet time during the day to refresh my spirit by reading scriptures, resting, and evaluating and assessing my obligations and goals. It occurred to me one day that my children may also need such a time, since they have so many activities in their lives. When they are home, they are now expected to spend some quiet time in their rooms while I enjoy my meditation time.

Listen for Answer

It is important to teach children how to listen for an answer to a prayer. If they don't relax to take a few moments of quiet time after praying, they may be cutting off half the communication. I tell them that praying is like talking to Heavenly Father on the telephone. If they don't take time to listen for an answer, then they are hanging up the phone on Heavenly Father.

I Will Do My Share

We want our children to understand that Heavenly Father will not answer our prayers the way we want them answered unless we are willing to sacrifice and do what we can to bring about our desires. For example, when we pray for blessings on the missionaries, we ask our children to provide some of those blessings in the form of small contributions of money, little gifts, and sincere letters to those they know.

CHURCH ATTENDANCE

Church or Chores
When a child says he doesn't want to go to church, my husband and I say, "Oh, that's quite all right. Since you won't be keeping the Sabbath holy anyway, you can wash all the windows in the house (or wash the car or weed the yard)." As soon as he hears this, he's quite ready for church!

"Do I Have to Go?"
One time when I heard a child complain about "having" to go to church, I was impressed by his grandmother's wise counsel. She told him that we are very much like a bucket with holes: it leaks water and needs to be constantly refilled. If we fail to attend church, our bucket runs dry of spiritual food and is empty until it's filled again. We never want to be empty, do we? Then we must continue to go to church and replenish our spiritual supply.

Why Bother?
Sometimes I wonder why I bother to go to church at all, since I spend the entire time hassling with my baby or preschoolers. I'm either walking the halls with the baby or whispering corrections to the others, so that I never hear more than clipped sentences here or there. I have to

remember that the reason I'm at church isn't always to get information. More importantly, I'm giving my children proper training in behavior at church and attitudes toward the Sabbath. This is the season for training; there will be future seasons for other purposes.

Setting an Example

"How can I get my son to go to the youth meetings?" one inactive mother once asked. "By your coming to Sunday School," I answered. "I just don't see how my going to Sunday School will get him to his meetings," she responded. She failed to see the principle of example in teaching her son. If we want our children to go to church, then we must go ourselves.

Too Noisy?

When a child has to be taken out of sacrament meetings, we let him know that he's not yet big enough to stay in the meeting with the rest of the family. When he is quiet all through the meeting and can stay, we compliment him and let him know he's growing up.

During the Sacrament

To keep the children quiet and to train them to properly take the sacrament, I tell them to talk to Heavenly Father while it is being passed. Then I bow my head in silent prayer, indicating that I'm not open to any whispered messages.

Keeps Them Quiet

I have given my preschoolers their own copies of the scriptures, even though they don't know how to read. They bring them to church each Sunday and "read" them by flipping the pages during sacrament meeting. This not only gets them in the habit of bringing their scriptures to church, but it also keeps them quiet during the meetings.

Picture Will Help

When my daughter was to give a talk in Sunday School before she knew how to read, I gave her a recipe card with drawings on it to remind her of what she was to say.

FORTY-TWO THINGS TO DO ON SUNDAY

What Can We Do on Sunday, Mom?

1. Find a well-known song and change the words to it. If the words describe your family or express love to Heavenly Father, you can sing it during family home evening.

2. Go through old *Friend* magazines or family home evening manuals. There are many stories or games you may enjoy playing or reading—or plan to present them to your family during family home evening.

3. Make lists about yourself:

"I wish I could . . ."

"I wish I hadn't done . . ."

"The things I like about myself are . . ."

"What I would like to change about myself . . ."

4. Write a letter to a friend, a grandparent, an aunt or uncle, a cousin, or a missionary. Include a drawing showing how you feel about the person to whom you are writing.

5. Plan and prepare to teach a hymn to the others during family home evening. Make a visual chart with pictures to help the little ones follow.

6. Copy genealogy sheets. Make your own book of remembrance. Study pictures of your ancestors and prepare a discussion on them for family home evening.

7. Record your weekly activities and feelings in a journal or on tape.

8. Make up a "Mormonism" on tape or paper, such as, "A scripture a day keeps the darkness away," or "Happiness is being LDS."

9. Write a scriptural message in Morse code or your own code to be deciphered during family home evening.

10. Check out magazines, filmstrips, or records from the meetinghouse library. Use them!

11. Visit or call an elderly neighbor. Tape-record his or her life history.

12. Make up a game using the scriptures as a theme.

13. With parental permission, offer to arrange and mount family photographs in an album. Share the joy of memories with a little brother or sister.

14. Set goals for yourself: "I will pick up my toys, without being asked, at least two times this week." "I will read the scriptures for five minutes each day." "I will count to ten when I feel like yelling."

15. Write a creative story about the life of baby Jesus, or a home that is a bit of heaven, or your premortal existence, or you as a mother/father, or living without the gospel.

16. Cut pictures from old magazines. Make a visual aids file for family home evening. Folders can be made by stapling two pieces of construction paper together and labeling "Families," "Food," "Work," "Teenagers," "Activities," and so on.

17. Glue a picture onto a piece of cardboard and then cut it up as a puzzle. Each piece could have an instruction on it to be done while the family puts the puzzle together:

—Give Mom a kiss.
—Give sister a compliment on her behavior.
—Rub or scratch Dad's back.
—Change the baby's diaper.

18. Prepare a simple Sabbath day meal or dessert.

19. Collect missionary tracts and arrange them in a folder

to be handed out to nonmembers or used as supplemental material for family home evening lessons.

20. Draw pictures representing your many blessings.

21. Interview your mother or father. Ask: "What is your favorite color? hymn? Church president?" "What is the first thing you remember as a child?" "What happened on your first date? first day at school? wedding day?" Record the answers and make copies for other family members.

22. Scramble letters of words that pertain to the family home evening lesson. Give each family member a copy and see who can unscramble them first.

22. Draw cartoons that tell a story. Show what Mr. Good Guy will do as contrasted with what Mr. Selfish would do in the same situation.

24. Read a scripture story and tell it to your little brother or sister.

25. Draw pictures of a happy face and a sad face. Ask your little brother or sister what he/she thinks made the face sad or happy, or make a list of the things that make you sad or happy.

26. Make a family home evening "duties" chart, or a work-assignment chart for the family.

27. Using cardboard, create your own scriptural paper doll (Ruth, Naomi, Mary, Sariah, etc.). Make clothes for it out of old scraps of materials or colored paper.

28. Create your own inspirational radio program, complete with advertisements, stories, music, and inspirational thoughts on tape.

29. Solve one of your problems by searching the scriptures for an answer. Pray about the problem and then let the book fall open, or use the Topical Guide or index in the back of the Bible to find specific topics and scriptural references. If you extend your faith, you will find the answer.

30. Memorize a scripture, Article of Faith, or the books of the Bible in order. Make up a song by putting them to a familiar tune.

31. If you don't already have one, create a family flag, complete with a motto, picture, and family name. You might consult with other family members before you finish it.

32. Make up your own riddles:

"How is the celestial kingdom like water?" (pure, refreshing, quenches thirst for love)

"What do the stars tell us about Heavenly Father?" (ordered, powerful, immense, lovely)

"How are the scriptures like eyeglasses?" (help us to see things we can't see on our own)

"How is the gospel like a pair of shoes?" (protects us from rocks of evil and takes us to Heavenly Father, step by step)

33. Plan to tell a scripture story to your little brothers or sisters. Make puppets out of paper bags. Cut a head out of construction paper, glue it on the bottom of a bag, and then draw the body on the remainder of the bag. Slip your hand into the bag and move the head while you talk for the puppet.

34. Collect common items found around your house—rubber bands, paper clips, toothpicks, cotton balls, construction paper, yarn, glue, crayons—and see what you can create.

35. Make name cards for family members to put on their bedroom doors, on the table, or on seats where they are to sit during dinner or family home evening. Design each letter so that it represents a character trait of the individual. For instance, a letter could have flames around it to show strength, flowers for gentleness, happy faces for joy, or hearts for love.

36. Make awards for members of your family, to be

presented during family home evening. Examples: "Best ten-year-old," "Most cheerful family member," "Best mother." A tiny paper plate could be used as a badge.

37. Make a gift for the bishop, your Sunday School teacher, or Mom and Dad. Write or type scriptures and thoughts on index cards for them to carry along to learn in quiet moments. Make a set for yourself, too. You might place some of them above the sink, on the bathroom mirror, on a door, or on the family bulletin board.

38. Ask your parents for some spare photos of family members. Then make a family tree on which you glue heads cut from old photos. Put Mom and Dad on the trunk and each child on a different branch. Grandparents can be on the roots.

39. Make bookmarks to be used in the scriptures. Take drawings or scriptural quotations and cover with clear Contact paper. These bookmarks make nice presents.

40. Make your own scrapbook about tithing, the Word of Wisdom, temples, missions, or Church presidents. Include pictures, talks, stories, and parents' testimonies or experiences.

41. Write a talk on one of the above topics, to be given during family home evening or in a meeting.

42. Plan a party for a Church president's birthday. Find stories or pictures about the president, and present an invitation to each member of your family. Tell each one about the president and have each give him an immaterial gift, such as a promise to improve in one way.

SABBATH ACTIVITIES

Felt Cutouts
Give each family member some felt to make cutouts for a story he'll invent. Have him present it on the flannel board during Sunday quiet time or family home evening.

Scriptural Blanks
Our children enjoy playing the "blank, blank" game on the Sabbath. Find a scripture, either well-known or not so well-known, and ask for players to fill in the blank. Examples:

"For whom the Lord loveth he ____________; even as a father the son in whom he delighteth." (See Proverbs 3:12.)

"For the commandment is a _________; and the law is ________; and reproofs of instruction are the way of life." (See Proverbs 6:23.)

Concentration
Make up your own memory game with either scriptural pairs or picture pairs. (You might use pictures of the beautiful things Heavenly Father has created, or discarded photographs of family members.) The object of the game is to try to match the pairs, which are mixed together and placed face down.

Letters in Design

Pick a word from the scriptures or a value you particularly want to emphasize, such as *charity*. Create your own decorative logo or design with the letters and hang it on your bedroom door as a reminder of that value.

Sequential Steps

Scriptural stories occur in sequence. Using cardboard or typing paper, draw a story: one episode on one page, the next on another, and so forth. Mix the pages up and ask someone to put them in order, telling the story as he organizes them.

Make a Machine

Invent and create your own machine using nuts, bolts, rubber bands, paper clips, glue, buttons, dials, or whatever materials you can find useful. Ideas: scripture-memory machine, obedience machine, preaching-the-gospel machine, instant-perfection machine.

Sandbox Picturama

We created a "picturama" that the children use on Sunday for their amusement and instruction. We filled a box with sand and asked the children to make a setting of Nephi's travels. We used the following to make it come to life:

Tiny boxes—house in Jerusalem
Small twigs—trees
Pipe cleaners—people and animals
Small hinges—brass plates
Pebbles—pathway and cave
Scraps of material—tents

Mirror—water
Moss—grass
If we allow the children to use their imaginations, they can think of more tiny items that work well for different scriptural stories.

Matching Game
Match each statement in the left-hand column below with the correct answer selected from the list in the right-hand column.

1. *Who* hath said in his heart there is no God? (Psalm 14:1)
2. *What* declares the glory of God? (Psalm 19:1)
3. *What* are like the chaff which the wind driveth away? (Psalm 1:4)
4. In *whom* is all the Lord's delight? (Psalm 16:3)
5. *Who* shall ascend into the hill of the Lord? (Psalm 24:3-5)
6. *What* is to be desired more than gold? (Psalm 19:1-10)

a. fool
b. the heavens
c. the ungodly
d. the pure in heart
e. the saints
f. rock and fortress
g. mercy and truth
h. the judgments of the Lord
i. the meek

7. *Who* shall eat and be satisfied? (Psalm 22:26)
8. *What* are the paths of the Lord? (Psalm 25:10)
9. The Lord is *what?* (Psalm 18:2)

Sunday Letter-Writing Club

We have a family club that meets every Sunday afternoon. Our teenage daughter, the president, gives us the names of those to whom we will write letters. The secretary, our ten-year-old, provides us with the writing material, which may be anything from lunch bags to the backs of homework papers. The treasurer provides us with the necessary stamps. We have written to investigators, missionaries, grandparents, aunts and uncles, and people in our former or current ward. We write either group letters or individual letters, depending upon our assignments from the president.

Sabbath-Day Play

Such toys as miniature wooden people, blocks, construction games, and even paper dolls can be tied into the Sabbath. Building Noah's ark, destroying the walls of Jericho, or reenacting Nephi's family's adventures can promote knowledge and faith.

7

FAMILY HOME EVENING

Every effort we can make
to foster meaningful close relationships
will help the home serve as
a sanctuary from evil
and become a source of strength
to each family member.
In our home evenings
and other positive family experiences
we can fill our souls with the things of God,
thus leaving no room for evil
to find a place in our hearts and minds.
(President Joseph Fielding Smith.)

A FAMILY TIME

What Do I Do?

I made a duties chart on a piece of plywood covered with burlap. The flower pots and flowers are made of felt. Letters for the names are alphabet macaroni, glued onto the felt with white glue. The flowers (on popsicle sticks) are moved from pot to pot to indicate who has what responsibilities for family home evening.

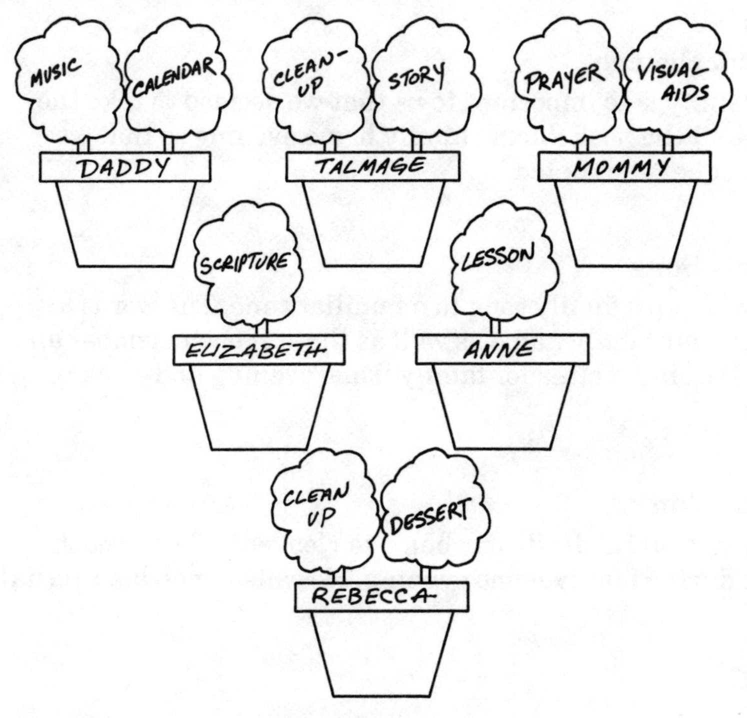

Sunday Afternoons
We have our family home evening lessons on Sunday afternoon. We feel a definite spiritual increase in our moods after attending church in the morning. We discuss what we learned in our respective classes, and have discovered the amazing correlation efforts from Salt Lake City. We also report on articles from the Church publications. This helps us to read the magazines more and increases our personal spirituality.

We're Having Home Evening!
Our family designed a family flag with colors, motto, and symbols representing our family goals and achievements. We display it on our front door on the Sabbath and when we're holding family home evening.

Do Not Disturb
Our family is so important to us that we decided to take the phone off the hook during family home evening so that we will not be interrupted.

Family Song
We made up a family song to a familiar tune. The words include our family name as well as those of each member and pets. We sing it often for family home evening and on car rides.

Dedication
My dad would dedicate our home to Heavenly Father each week during family home evening. He called upon his Eternal

Father's help in raising us and humbly admitted that he knew he made errors. We felt his sincerity in trying to be a parent who was in tune, and we silently confirmed his prayer for a blessed home.

Love Coupons

After receiving love-coupon books from my children for Father's Day, with promises to complete certain chores for me, I decided to give each of the children a book from me. For family home evening, I presented them with coupons good for:

—evening ride alone
—ice cream cone
—back rub for fifteen minutes
—story
—game of catch
—day of making your bed or doing your dishes
—trip to the grocery store to spend fifty cents on anything they desire

ATTENTION GETTERS

Use the Manual

The family home evening manuals are inspired of the Lord! We find that when we follow the lessons, after selecting them to suit the needs of our family, we are much more successful than when we make up our own lessons. However, we have added zest to them by thinking of special ways to get the children's attention. The following are attention-getting ideas:

1. Play music—hymns, marches, Primary songs. If parents just start to sing or march to the music, the children will join them.

2. Put an odd object in the center of the living room floor. If a wheelbarrow, a lamp, a stack of books, or a loaf of bread is placed in an unusual spot, the children will take notice and want to find out what the lesson will be.

3. Disappear, leaving notes with clues to lead the children to where you are going to hold the lesson. Try unusual places: on the hill behind your house, in the garage, on your bed, in the bathroom, or in the car.

4. Wear a costume, such as a hat, apron, uniform, or feather, that will tie in with the lesson. Use your imagination. Or have a neighbor dress up as the visiting pixie, offering rewards for good behavior or leaving messages containing the main idea of the lesson.

5. Wrapped presents always catch the eye of the children. Inside, write directions concerning the lesson: "Mary, relate an experience you had when you felt unhappy." "Johnny, why do we have family rules?"

6. Blow up balloons and scatter them all over the house or living room. Inside each balloon place a note containing an important message of the lesson or a question for the participants.

7. A pile of coins or a twenty-dollar bill on the floor of the living room will always arouse interest.

8. Ask a thought-provoking question: "What would you do if . . ."

9. From the scriptures, pretending to be King Benjamin, a psalmist, or Joseph Smith, read the words of that person with feeling and enthusiasm.

10. Relate a personal experience of something that happened to you when you were younger.

11. Pick a spiritual quotation and read it over and over until everyone joins in to say it with you.

12. Tell a joke that pertains to the lesson material.

13. Recite a poem. Rewrite one to include family names.

14. Use diagrams; posters or illustrations are helpful in creating interest.

15. Cut cartoons from the newspaper or make one up.

16. Make a statement that opposes your views and have the children refute it. Sample statements might include these: "Paying tithing is a waste of time." "It doesn't hurt to smoke pot." "Dating before sixteen should be allowed." "Children should be seen and not heard."

17. Invite a guest speaker to tape comments pertaining to the lesson. This person might be a relative who lives far away or the bishop, stake president, or patriarch.

18. Have a scavenger hunt. Collect certain items from

around the house. Each person has to explain how these items tie in with the lesson.

19. Use puppets or dolls. "Talking" can create a mood of joy!

20. Pictures or works of art draw attention.

21. Give each person a ticket that tells him to come to the meeting. Airline, movie, or railroad tickets work nicely.

22. Blindfold each person and lead him to the meeting place.

23. Allow no talking. Have the teacher teach the first part of the lesson in pantomime. Have family members determine the meaning.

LESSON IDEAS

Age-span Problem

There are many solutions to the problem of trying to teach both teens and preschoolers. Here are four suggestions:

1. Ask questions on the individual's own level. The younger ones learn from listening to the older ones.
2. Give the younger children activities, such as related puzzles or drawing assignments, to work on while you teach the older children.
3. Have one parent teach the older children while the other teaches the younger ones. Break up as in Sunday School.
4. Teach the older ones after the younger ones are in bed.

Church Magazines

Our children take turns reporting on an article or story from one of the Church magazines or newspaper. This is an honor and encourages participation and interest in family home evening.

Conference Tapes

We enjoy listening to general conference talks on tape during our family meetings. When a talk is finished, we discuss the highlights and how to apply the principles to our lives. If children are too young to listen to the entire talk, excerpts might be played.

Testimonies

Occasionally we'll have a family testimony meeting in which everyone participates.

Articles of Faith

We've memorized all the Articles of Faith by repeating a particular one at the beginning of each meeting for one month before continuing with another.

Children Know the Answers!

We allowed our children to participate in a panel discussion. My husband and I asked them questions, which they answered with their own opinions and thoughts. We were delighted and surprised with their knowledge and good sense.

Jet Ride to Celestial Kingdom

We presented to our children a simulated jet ride to the various degrees of glory. Using the intercom system for directions from the pilot, we told them we were going on a special flight. They all had to remain blindfolded until they arrived at the "celestial kingdom." We began in a dark room with loud, clanging music, to represent the "telestial kingdom." They didn't want to stay there, so we moved on to the "terrestrial kingdom." It was just an average room, a little lighter than the other, but not fully lit. The "celestial kingdom," however, was fully lit, and in it were pictures of all our departed relatives. We then served the family's favorite treat, ice cream sundaes.

Family History
Dad showed us a chart containing the names of our ancestors, who were from Mexico, Germany, England, and Ireland. We each picked a country, studied its geography and culture, and then reported on it during family home evening.

Personal Baby Books
Mother managed to save all the information for our baby books, but she never got around to filling them. On one family home evening, she presented the material to each child and let him compile it as he saw fit.

Toss for Direction
Place scriptures or directions pertaining to the lesson in the sections of an empty egg carton. Then have each family member toss a bean, button, or coin into it. They are to follow whatever instructions they find in the section they hit.

The Savior Is Listening
One night Dad surprised us with a tape that he had secretly recorded during dinner. He asked us to listen to it and decide whether or not we were ready for a visit from the Savior. He asked each of us what we heard; we all agreed that it was *selfishness* more than anything else. He reminded us that Heavenly Father hears all the time, and warned us that he'll record us again sometime to see if we've improved.

Questions for Dad

We have enjoyed family home evening much more since we introduced "Dad's Question Box." During the week, we jot down any question we may have concerning the gospel or other matters that bother us. We then place these in the question box, from which Dad will draw two or three, depending on the time. He will answer them, using scriptural passages for support. The older children sometimes stump him, but in such cases he'll come back with the answer the next week. Generally he does quite well, gaining the respect and admiration of all. The older boys are now planning to see if they can do as well as he does. They want a scripture chase with him!

Who Am I?

Dad will often test our knowledge of the scriptures by playing "Who Am I?" with us. He'll give us clues by pantomiming the actions of the character or by stating facts about him. He will give one clue, wait to see if we can guess, and then go on to another until someone finally guesses correctly. The winner then gets to pantomime a person for us. We've really sharpened our knowledge of the scriptures in this manner. An example of the clues may be as follows:

1. I came to childless parents, who were told by an angel that I would deliver the Israelites from the Philistines.
2. One day I killed a lion with my bare hands.
3. I also caught three hundred foxes and tied them together tail to tail. I then fastened a torch to them and turned them loose to burn cornfields.
4. I was not wise but I was very strong, so strong that I killed a thousand men with a jawbone, when they tried to take me captive.

5. I met my downfall when I fell in love with a lady who learned the secret that would rob me of my strength.

Who am I? (Samson)

Scripture Games

Each week we assign a scripture story for the entire family to read. It may be the story of Job, or of Moses and the bullrushes, or the adventure of Nephi and his brothers getting the brass plates from Laban. Even the youngest are expected to know it by the next family home evening; someone will read the children's version to them. When we meet again, we have a little quiz at the beginning of the meeting. We usually rotate the honor of writing the questions for the quiz from member to member, including Mom and Dad.

Pixie Dust to Wish

During one family home evening, Dad brought a covered woven basket into the room. He told us that there was invisible pixie dust in it that would, in the world of make-believe, cause whatever we wished to appear.

Each of us then wrote down an item, tangible or intangible, that we wished were in the basket. Mom wished for three more hours in the day, while Sam wished for someone to write his science report. Dad wished for happy, obedient children, while I wished for a new dress.

Dad said that he would help Sam formulate an idea for his report and find some helpful books if we, as children, would be obedient and offer to do Mom's chores, in order to give her more time in the day. Know what Mom said she would do with her extra time? You guessed it—make me a new dress! That pixie dust really works.

Family Preparedness

After living on our food storage and carrying water for six weeks, as a result of an Alaskan earthquake, our family has an acute awareness of disasters. We converted our guest closet, which is next to our front door, into an emergency locker. It contains all of our sleeping bags, several items of small camping gear, a shopping bag full of bandages, and a large tackle box with our first-aid supplies. Each of us has a flight bag packed with extra clothes, toiletries, and personal survival items. We have also invested in a large tent, camp table, and lamps, which we plan to store outside the house, so that in the event of an emergency, we have a supplemental supply.

ACTIVITIES

Who Are You?
Choose four to six players or dolls to represent scriptural characters, such as Sarah, Rachel, Samson, or David. Then have the other players close their eyes while those representing scriptural characters change places. When they are rearranged, those who are seated try to name the characters in their new order, in addition to making a statement about the life of each character.

Presidents of the Church
Presidents of the Church, the Church's student manual for Religion 345, is a wonderful source of information about the Church presidents. We play a game in which we give incidents from the lives of various presidents. Everyone is then asked to identify the presidents. Examples:

"Stricken by disease at age seven, he was left lame and limping for years, years filled with farm work and family moves." (Joseph Smith, p. 27.)

"Instead of crying over our sufferings, as some seem inclined to do, I would rather tell a good story, and leave the crying to others. I do not know that I have ever suffered; I do not realize it. Have I not gone without eating and not half clad? Yes, but that was not suffering. I was used to that in my youth. I used to work in the woods logging and driving team, summer and winter, not half clad, and with insufficient food until my stomach would ache, so that I am used to all this, and have had no suffering." (Brigham Young, p. 63.)

The only president who was not a native-born American. (John Taylor, p. 85.)

"I had the administration of angels while holding the office of a priest. I had visions and revelations. I traveled thousands of miles. I baptized men, though I could not confirm them because I had not the authority to do it." (Wilford Woodruff, p. 109.)

Jacob and Rachel

Everyone stands in a circle around two players, whom we call Jacob and Rachel. Jacob, who is blindfolded, says, "Rachel, where art thou?" Rachel must then answer, "Here I am, Jacob." She tries to escape him within the ring each time, but she must answer when asked. When she is caught, she then is blindfolded and a different "Jacob" is selected to answer her questions. If you have a family of boys, the names Nephi and Lehi could be used, or Ruth and Naomi for girls.

Name That Tune

Someone sits at the piano and plays little snatches of well-known hymns. Each family member attempts to identify them before anyone else does. Eventually we will try to identify the hymns after only two or three notes are played.

Cooperation

To teach our children cooperation, we will have them play this game: Two children stand back to back and lock arms.

They then race against another pair or race against their own last time record. When Mother and Father do this, everyone is amused!

Picture Game

I cut a picture of something pertaining to the family home evening lesson into twenty-four squares. I then number the backs of the squares from one to twelve, repeating the numbers so that I have two sets, numbering from one to twelve. We then mix up the pieces and place them with the number side down, so that we see a scrambled picture. We turn over two pieces at a time, trying to match numbers. When the numbers match, we keep those two pieces to build the picture. If they don't match, we turn them back over, leaving them in their original spot. The game continues until all the pieces are matched and the picture is completed.

Guess Who?

Each family member is given a list of the following objects. They are to name the people that these objects suggest:

1. Burning bush (Moses)
2. Coat of many colors (Joseph)
3. Pair of animals (Noah)
4. Locks of hair (Samson)
5. Brass plates (Nephi)
6. Sheaves of wheat (Ruth and Naomi)
7. Tower (King Benjamin)
8. Slingshot (David)
9. Golden calf (Children of Israel)
10. Temple (Solomon)

Initials

Each person draws from a hat a slip of paper with the initials of another member of the family. Each is then asked a series of questions about the person whose initials are on his paper; the questions must be answered in three words, beginning with the initials in their proper order. For example:

1. To whom does this HJG paper belong? (Heather Jean Giesea)
2. What is her character? (Humble, Joyful, Gleeful)
3. What scriptural characters does she admire? (Hannah, Job, Gabriel)
4. What commandment does she obey? (Honor Just Grandparents)
5. What does she think about the Church? (Handles Joyful Giants)

Get in Shape

We really laughed hard when we had an exercise evening for activity night. We decided we needed to become inspired in physical fitness awareness.

Foreign Country Night

We invited a family from San Salvador to attend our family home evening. In advance, we learned all we could about their country and then decorated the house in honor of it. We prepared their native food and asked them to share information about their country. They enjoyed the evening, and we felt it was a positive experience.

Classified Ad

FOR SALE: One thirteen-year-old man. Does work and babysits for only a small plate of food. Knows how to clean house and can save you money by balancing your books. Does light yard work and likes animals. Showers regularly. If interested, call GOOD GUY.

FOR SALE: Attractive 37-year-old man. Good income. Loves children, old Porsches, new Mercedes. Actively involved in church and lives a good life. Very affectionate. Loves white, sandy beaches and clear blue water. Call anytime.

FOR SALE: Eleven-year-old girl. Easy to love. Fun to be with. Never lies. Always ready to help out. Very clean and pure. Doesn't get involved with bad people or bad things. Is very sweet and considerate. Always awakens with a great big smile.

FOR SALE: I love dogs and I'm good at doing housework. I eat a lot, but am not fat. Love to swim. Blue eyes. Take a shower every Sunday. Attend church. Don't drink or smoke. What more could you want from a ten-year-old boy?

The above are samples of the "classified ads" our family wrote. To help build self-esteem in each other, Dad had us each write an ad pretending another member of the family was for sale. The rules were that we could only take five minutes to write it, and everything stated must be positive. At the end of the time, we each read our ad aloud, and the others were asked to guess whom it was about.

Alternate: Write an ad for yourself, or honor one person with ads from everyone.

8

FAMILY TRADITIONS

We can guide, direct,
and prune a tender sprout,
and it inclines to our direction,
if it is wisely and skillfully applied.
So, if we surround a child
with healthy and salutary influences,
give him suitable instruction
and store his mind with truthful tradition,
may be that will direct his feet
in the way of life.

(Brigham Young, Journal of Discourses *9:248.)*

FAMILY UNITY

Family Flower

Our family has chosen the gardenia as our family flower. It is the kind of flower Mom had in her bridal bouquet. Whenever there is a special holiday or family reunion, we have gardenias in the house.

Family Motto

We picked a motto for our family banner, which we attach to the front door during family home evening. It states "Perfection or Bust!" Another family's motto is "As for our house, we will serve the Lord."

Family Flag

One family has a flag with all their handprints and the words "Making Memories" on it. They fly it on their tent when they camp and display it in the car window when they travel.

Where Are You?

Another family has special, brightly colored T-shirts printed with their surname. They wear them whenever they're in large crowds so that Mom and Dad can find lost children easily.

Missionary Letter Journal

We have devised a method to save time for ourselves and our missionary son. We write records of our daily activities on journal paper and then mail them to each other. The missionary keeps the family records and returns home with them, and the family keeps the missionary records for him in a journal. Both letter-writing and journal-keeping are finished in one effort!

Prayer

We all hold hands around the dinner table while we pray. It adds to family loving and also keeps the little ones' hands out of the food. We also hold hands during family prayer; it unites us and keeps everyone still.

Family Pixie Pals

Our ward has started a tradition that has great impact on the feelings of one family for another. For two weeks in December we secretly leave surprises on the doorstep of another family, selected by a drawing of names. Some families use a Twelve-Days-of-Christmas theme for gift selections. "Pixie Pals" are then revealed at our ward Christmas party.

Love Spreads

I started making up love notes and placing them in my husband's pockets, socks, shaving can, shirts, notebooks, or even on his calendar at work. Now each member of the family will find little notes from the others.

What's New?
The Martin family prepares a newsletter, in newspaper format, to send to their friends and relatives. Each member of the family contributes to it, and it serves a fine purpose.

A RECORD-KEEPING FAMILY

Expandable Binders

Our children's favorite journal is an expandable press binder filled with loose filler paper. Each binder contains one year's worth of cards, letters, selected schoolwork, and photos.

Hospital Stay

I helped my son compile a scrapbook in memory of a stay in the hospital. We included everything from a copy of the bills to pictures and autographs of the doctors, as well as cards from visitors. It gave him something to do during his recovery, and the finished product will fit nicely into his book of remembrance.

Move-a-Log

When we moved into a new area, each child compiled a "Move-a-log" to become part of his book of remembrance. I encouraged them to place pictures of their new neighborhood, school, parks, city hall, and church building beside those of the old. A list of the names of old friends, with a word and a picture from each, can add happy memories to the book.

File of Memories

With eight children, we find it difficult to keep track of all their major achievements, cute sayings, and clever anecdotes. However, it has been easier since we started to keep file cards handy. In a file box, we have sections labeled with each child's name. We just add to their files as needed. Now we have quite a lot of information on each child.

Journal Entries

Occasionally I take a child's journal, with his permission, and make a nice entry about that particular child. I try to record memories of the last few weeks and the strengths I see in him, as well as expressions of love and praise.

Memory Gallery

You can create a memory gallery by framing marriage licenses, baptism certificates, and other items of interest. One father framed a telegram he sent his son when he was away on a trip. Another daughter framed her father's old keys. A child enjoys seeing his work framed and hanging on his bedroom wall. School drawings, from kindergarten on up, show a child's artistic growth and look handsome in a gallery on the wall.

Baby's Memoirs

We have started a journal for our baby. In it, we are recording our trips and vacations with her and how she acted and reacted to new people and surroundings. When she gets older, we'll turn this book over to her so she can keep it herself. You might also record birthdays, special occasions, special friends, moves, and so forth.

FAMILY REUNION IDEAS

1. Hold the reunion in a campground over a three-day weekend.

2. Have a testimony meeting.

3. Elect officers to serve on a yearly basis:

President—chief organizer.

Vice-president—assistant organizer; will be president next year.

Secretary—in charge of correspondence and record-keeping.

Treasurer—in charge of missionary funds and expenses.

Genealogy representative—gathers and distributes information.

Activities chairman—plans group activities.

4. Everyone is asked to contribute baked goods, crafts, arts, or services to sell at a bazaar. The money goes to a genealogy and missionary fund. Each missionary receives one hundred dollars when he leaves for a mission.

5. Have a likeness of each family member appliquéd or drawn on a fabric square. Combine these squares into a quilt, to be raffled off or presented to the oldest living family member.

6. Each immediate family contributes a banner, which is joined with others to form a huge flag. The flag is flown during the reunion.

7. Make available a book filled with pictures of the ancestor, which families can order copies of. Or have each person stand up to tell something about the ancestor. These tributes may be recorded on tape and then distributed to all.

8. Choose a familiar tune and have each family make up at least one verse for a family song. The members of the family may be introduced within those verses, as well as details about where they live and interesting facts about them.

9. Each couple shares with the family some highlights from their courtship. Someone keeps a record of the statements for a book to be distibuted among the members.

10. Identify family members by name tags, T-shirts, or clothing color. Some families give each member a scarf. You might also select a different color to identify each generation.

11. Plan competition between different generations or age groups. A diaper-pinning race between fathers, a singing contest, or a dance display can be most enjoyable. Other fun activities: licorice chew, tug-of-war, wheelbarrow races.

12. Assign meals by families. One family each day will cook for the others, on a rotation basis.

13. Give family awards. Make badges or blue ribbons for the newest member of the family, the oldest, the family with the most children, best sense of humor, and so on.

14. Have the older family members serve a fancy candlelight dinner to the teenagers. Each teenager draws the name of a cousin of the opposite sex as his/her dinner partner.

15. A "junk-food" breakfast delights young and old. Another breakfast idea is to hide decorated eggs and have everyone hunt for his meal.

16. Plan an arts-and-crafts time for the little children. You might have them make banks in which to save money for the next reunion. Cans covered with burlap work well; Mom

and Dad get a big one, while each child makes one for himself. One year, we blew out eggs, cooked and ate the insides for breakfast, then decorated the shells with faces and hats. Another time we collected sticks representing members of the family and put little eyes and mouths on them.

17. Have a talent night in which each family performs a routine. Examples: song with actions, such as "The Three Little Pigs," a wrestling match between couples, tumbling exercises.

18. Each family is in charge of teaching everyone a new song, to be sung around the table, before bedtime, on walks, and so on.

19. Have a family parade. Costumes, songs, and props might be developed around a particular theme: "Countries of Ancestors," "Happiness Is Family Activities," "Display of Family Crest."

20. Plan a scavenger hunt. Go around the neighborhood to collect items on a list.

21. Prepare an agenda of activities and send it to each family before the reunion, so that preparations can be made in advance.

22. Take pictures of each family group and of the entire group.

23. Ask families to bring short selections from home movies.

24. Invite a guest speaker to give an inspirational talk.

25. Have coins, candy, and small trinkets mixed in straw for the little children to collect.

GENERAL HOLIDAYS

Holiday Eggs

While coloring Easter eggs, we came up with egg-coloring ideas for other holidays:

Red and white eggs—Valentine's Day
Orange eggs with pumpkin faces—Halloween
Red, white, and blue eggs—Fourth of July
Red and green eggs—Christmas

Poetry on Holidays

We read the following poems on the holidays indicated: "Concord Hymn" and "Paul Revere's Ride" on the Fourth of July; "The Landing of the Pilgrims" on Thanksgiving; "The Commemoration Ode" on Memorial Day; "Death of the Old Year" (Tennyson) on New Year's Eve; and "Tyger, Tyger, Burning Bright" (Blake) after a trip to the zoo.

Form a Word

Whenever we celebrate a holiday, we try to see how many words can be formed out of the letters in that holiday's name. We each make a list and then share them with the rest of the family.

EASTER

Saturday Egg Hunt
To solve the Easter/Sabbath-day problem, I started a yearly neighborhood Easter-egg hunt, held on the Saturday before Easter. In that way, we avoid the interference of the Easter Bunny on the Sabbath. Each neighbor will contribute candies or eggs for the hunt as well as their help.

Grass Beds for Eggs
A few weeks before Easter, we cut milk cartons in half and fill them with soil, then plant grass seed in them. By Easter the grass has grown out, and we put the cartons in decorative baskets to serve as beds for colored Easter eggs.

HALLOWEEN

No Pumpkins
Round oatmeal boxes can be used for jack-o'-lanterns. Our children carry them every Halloween while trick-or-treating. Draw eyes, nose, and mouth on one end and cut out as you would with a pumpkin. Paste Halloween cutouts on the outside for decoration. A flashlight placed inside gives it a jack-o'-lantern look.

Fireside Talk
After trick-or-treating, we sit around the fire in our costumes, sharing our night's adventures, while eating popcorn and collected candies.

Name Pumpkins
Before Halloween, when the pumpkins are little, go to a pumpkin patch. Have each child carve his name on a pumpkin, leaving it on the vine. As the pumpkin grows, the name gets bigger and bigger.

No Trick, Just Treats
We live in a rural farming community where most of the neighbors are elderly. I was concerned about Halloween,

because these kind neighbors wouldn't be prepared for my children's visit. After discussing the problem with my five children, ranging in age from one to ten, we came up with a plan that has far exceeded our expectations. Each year we prepare homemade foods and choose several neighbors to visit. The children still dress up, but they do not take sacks to the door. Instead, they greet our neighbors with a plate of treats and a "Happy Halloween!" They didn't receive treats in return at some houses the first year, but now, after four years, everyone looks forward to our visit, and the children receive more candy from ten homes than if they went to twenty or thirty in town. The warm expressions of appreciation, such as, "Why, we've never *received* a treat—how wonderful!" mean more to us than the candy.

THANKSGIVING

Piñata
Every Thanksgiving, we break open a piñata, either purchased or made from a balloon covered with flour-and-water paste and decorated with tissue paper. Nuts, coins, and candy fall out for the family to gather.

Visit from the Pixie
Since Mother has to work so diligently to prepare the Thanksgiving feast, members of our family decided to surprise her by getting up early in the morning to do chores, such as mopping the floors, peeling apples for the pie, or setting the table.

Prayer of Thanksgiving
The eldest member of our family has the honor of offering a special Thanksgiving prayer of thanks, which is said as we sit around the table holding hands.

Thanksgiving Story
We retell the story of the pilgrims before every Thanksgiving feast in our home. We also share pictures of the costumes of

the era, and of our ancestors who arrived in this country during that time.

Blessings Recalled
We have candelabra decorating the Thanksgiving table. Each member of the family is allowed to light one candle, while stating a blessing for which he is grateful.

Surprise!
We enjoy sharing our blessings with others on Thanksgiving, so we will leave something on doorsteps of our friends the night before. Desserts, homemade jams, nuts, or bundles of firewood are our tokens of love.

CHRISTMAS

Remembrances

Each year Mother prepares a special addition for each child's book of remembrance. She may include a special testimony, a life history, a picture pedigree chart, or additional family group sheets, along with update sheets.

Christmas Eve

We have a big, fancy meal on Christmas Eve, for which we use our best china. Every year my mother brings out a beautifully decorated birthday cake. This helps us remember whose birthday it is that we are celebrating.

Christmas Gifts for the Elderly

We like to give Christmas gifts to some of the older members of the ward. We will wrap up intangible gifts, written on cards, such as: "The Moore family will be at your house this Saturday from 8:00 A.M. to 3:00 P.M. Make a list of the things you need fixed around your house, and we'll do them." Additional ideas:

—Join you in playing chess or other games for an hour or two

—Pick you up for family home evening whenever you wish
—Weed your yard
—Write letters for you while you dictate
—Move furniture
—Plant shrubs
—Take you shopping
—Fix or cut your hair
—Let you talk to your sister or child long distance for as long as you like
—Drive you to the temple at your convenience
—Bring dinner to you for a week
—Tape your personal history while you dictate

Holiday Family Home Teaching

I take my entire family home teaching with me during the Christmas holidays. Everyone looks forward to this special visiting time.

Intangible Gifts

We ask each person in our family to make a list of the intangible gifts he would like to receive. For example:

1. The ability to speak in front of big crowds.
2. The ability to smile when everything seems dismal.
3. The courage to say what I think when everyone else is choosing the wrong.
4. The ability to recognize the still small voice.

We are then asked to choose which one we'll give ourselves to develop during the coming twelve months, so it won't be on our list next year.

Too Big

When I give a gift to the children that is too big to wrap, such as a bicycle, I find a miniature or a small picture and wrap it up before presenting the real thing.

Handprints on Grandmother's Apron

One of our grandmother's favorite Christmas aprons is one onto which we transferred our handprints. Each grandchild's handprint and name were drawn on with fabric crayon.

New Year's Wish

Each New Year, my dad would make a wish for each one of us, seal it in an envelope, and save it to be opened the following year. We used to eagerly anticipate that it would somehow come true during the year. If it didn't, then we'd make certain it did the next year.

BIRTHDAYS

Am I as Tall as Dad Was?
Each year on my birthday, Dad would paint a mark behind the kitchen door to indicate my height, making notations of my age and the date. Now my own children enjoy measuring themselves against my marks when we visit Grandma's house.

Ongoing Poem
We started a poem for each of our children on the day he or she was born. We add a verse or two at each birthday, including the highlights of growth and activities of the year.

I'll Miss Work for You
My husband takes a half-day off work when one of our children has a birthday. He devotes his full attention to the birthday child, letting him choose how he wants to spend the time.

Pickle Jar Present
Dad gives each of us a special treat on our birthdays. He saves his change all year round in a gallon pickle jar. The birthday

person gets to reach into the jar with one hand. Whatever he can grasp is his to keep.

Birthday Mural

Mom attaches a long sheet of butcher paper to the kitchen wall on the morning of a birthday. Party guests and members of the family then contribute drawings or words of praise in tribute to the birthday person. By the end of the day, the mural is complete.

Twelve-year-olds

My dad gave each of his sons a set of scriptures with "Elder" printed on them when each received the priesthood at the age of twelve. "Elder" was to remind us of our commitment to go on a mission. When the girls turned twelve, he gave them white leather scriptures printed with their names. These books were autographed with words such as these: "To my special daughter, who promised to stay clean and worthy of a temple marriage."

Traditional Gifts

In our family, as each child was baptized, he received a Bible. At thirteen, each girl received a pearl ring. When we were of high-school age, we would have one piece of luggage added at each birthday, so that we had a complete set in time for college.

Dinner with Dad

As each girl in our family became a teenager, she was taken out to dinner by Dad. This gave us time to be alone and to talk with him. It was also an opportunity to learn restaurant table manners—good practice for dating.

Gifts for Goals

In order to help our children reach goals, we traditionally give them certain gifts on certain birthdays. For instance:

8th birthday—diary

10th birthday—journal

12th birthday—Book of Remembrance

14th birthday on up—each girl receives an item to add to her hope chest; each boy receives missionary gifts. Both receive scriptures and Church books.

Birthday Favor Balls

Put party favors inside a "ball" by wrapping a favor in strips of crepe paper or yarn. Keep wrapping round and round until the ball is as big as you wish. Tape the end of the yarn. Your guests will enjoy the anticipation of unwrapping the ball to find the favor.

Favor Bags

My mother started a tradition for our birthdays. She would transfer our artwork onto fabric, which she then sewed into favor bags. We were very pleased to give a "gift of ourselves" to our guests, who had a permanent bag to use for storing their little toys.

SPIRITUAL

June Brides

Every June, we go to the temple to watch the brides come out for picture-taking. I know that when my girls feel the serenity and beauty of a temple wedding on the outside, it enhances their hopes of going inside one day.

Missionary Barrel

In our kitchen we have a "missionary barrel," into which members of our family will toss their extra pennies at the end of the day. It's surprising how quickly the money adds up.

Fasting

My husband and I fast once a week for our marriage. We realize that even our marriage could be threatened if we don't keep ourselves constantly striving for the closeness marriage brings.

NEW ADDITIONS

What Were You Doing?

With the birth of each niece and nephew in our family, I wrote a page or two in my journal describing members of the family—aunts, uncles, grandparents. I included a notation on where everyone was and what they were doing at the time of birth—"Your Uncle Kent is living in Provo, Utah, going to BYU." I also inserted a little about the baby's parent's background, including where they have lived and their feelings about the new arrival. This will be a special gift to them from me when they get older.

Baby Talk

My daughter will be able to listen to her baby sounds when she's grown, because we've been recording them on a tape we plan to preserve just for her. As she grows, we'll record her blessings, talks, confirmation, and other special occurrences. She's already fascinated at hearing her own voice on tape.

Blanket

Each time a great-grandchild is born, my grandmother crochets a blanket just for the baby. These are special as well as practical.

Growth Scale

For Christmas this year, I'm making each niece and nephew a "growth scale." It will be a scroll made of Pellon, seven feet long by eighteen inches wide, with feet and inches marked off. On each birthday the child will be able to mark off his height. Other information can also be added, such as the child's weight, his traced handprint, a sample of his handwriting, or his name. This scroll can be hung up on the wall in the child's room or brought out on birthdays. Cars, trucks, or planes made out of Pellon can be glued along the border for boys, flowers for girls.

Don't Leave Me Out

To involve the children in the arrival of a new baby, we have each child wrap a gift from himself, such as plastic pants, sleeper, or bottles, to be given to the new baby. Mom and Dad have a special gift wrapped for each child from the new baby, to be exchanged when the baby and Mom come home from the hospital.

MISCELLANEOUS

Memories
Bridal, funeral, or prom bouquets can be dried and placed under a glass dome to preserve them. Shadow boxes can show off collections of mementos, such as war or Scout medals.

Train Helps to Teach
I made a cardboard train to hang in my three-year-old son's room. Each car holds little slips of papers that he can pull out easily. On the slips, I put colors, numbers, letters, words, or songs. Before nap or bedtime, he selects one paper and we review it. He learns and has fun at the same time!

Traveling Notebook
I made a notebook strictly for use in the car. In it are finger plays, songs, stories, crafts, and learning games.

Car Travel
Listening to tapes has been the most quieting and enjoyable activity we've found for traveling. We enjoy storybook tapes, music, and the tapes that accompany children's scriptural picture books.

Waffles on Call
When teenagers at our home tire of an activity in the late evening, they make waffles. We have a waffle iron reserved especially for them.

Batch of Cookies
We save our margarine tubs to fill with cookie dough. We then freeze the dough until we're ready to deliver it to the elderly people in our ward. They can enjoy the luxury of freshly baked cookies at their convenience.

House-Warming Gift
When we have a friend who is building a new home or one who has just moved into an unlandscaped home, we take pictures of the home at each stage of completion. This series of photos makes a touching Christmas or house-warming gift.

What Will I Fix?
Whenever a young woman in our ward gets married, we give her a collection of our favorite recipes in a file.

Clothes Exchange
Once a year we have a neighborhood clothes exchange to which everyone brings cast-offs to trade.

Family Tree
An old oak tree in our yard has become a part of our family. If Dad has a meaningful piece of news to share, he'll whisper to each of us, "Meet me out by the family tree in five minutes." I

remember the feelings of eager anticipation as we waited for these meetings. Once he told us that our family would be able to go to Disneyland for a vacation. Another time he reported that Aunt Jane had broken her leg and needed our help. Occasionally I would be the only one asked to meet him there. Those times were special, because we'd just stretch out under the tree and have a leisurely talk.

Pictures by the Chair

I take pictures of our children each year standing beside an antique, high-back chair. It has become the measuring rod of the children's growth. I have found that if I let them hold their favorite toy, tension is eased and the picture turns out better.

Quilt Tells a Story

Mom made a quilt for my brother when he received his Eagle Scout award. All of his merit badges were sewn onto it as appliqués. In the center was an eagle that Mom designed and appliquéd.

Coat of Arms

Each member of the family, including Mom and Dad, is asked to draw his own personal coat of arms. Then the drawings can be colored and framed, or transferred onto fabric for a quilt, pillow cover, or wall hanging. They can be colored with liquid embroidery paints or stitched with embroidery floss, depending on the age or desire of the child. If each member of the family has his own pillow with his coat of arms, no one has to guess whose pillow hasn't been put away!

The coat of arms might include—
—a favorite color
—a favorite activity
—an inspirational scriptural passage
—a long-term goal
—a favorite motto
—something to represent a positive character trait

9

BEATING THE BLAHS!

Life gives to all the choice.
You can satisfy yourself
with mediocrity if you wish.
You can be common,
ordinary, dull, colorless;
or you can channel your life
so that it will be clean,
vibrant, progressive, useful,
colorful, rich.

(President Spencer W. Kimball.)

BEATING THE BLAHS!

Mental Security

Faith in god and a real faith in myself ensure the most success for me. Without my daily scripture study, time for myself, and communication with my Father, I become lost. Without a deep love for—and faith in—myself, I know the real meaning of fear. I put a lot of trust in this scripture: "For God hath not given us the spirit of fear; but of power, and of love, and of a sound mind." (2 Timothy 1:7.)

Taking Care of Myself

Heavenly Father wants me to learn how to take care of myself. Many mothers think it's noble to continually put everyone's needs above their own. In reality, taking care of myself is my number one responsibility, and it's a job that can be done only by me. To be able to give the quality of love I desire to give and to provide happy experiences for my family, I must keep myself physically and mentally fit. This means I must be aware of my needs and willing to find time and ways to fulfill them.

Wait until Noon

For years I've had a particularly hard time getting up and going in the morning. Sometimes I find it difficult to break through the morning darkness with enough enthusiasm to face the day. Years ago I would just roll over, sleep a lot, or merely "slug" through the day. For over a year and a half now, I have been changing this. I still experience the morning "blahs," but I force myself up and out of bed early. I head straight for the bathroom and don't come out till I'm showered, dressed, and groomed. While I'm showering and getting ready, I give myself a pep talk. I tell myself over and over, "I will not judge this day until noon. Until then, I will work as if it were going to be a good day. If at noon it is awful, I will allow myself to give in." I've yet to have a day that has found me giving up!

Success by the Year

If I write just one page a day in my journal, I will have a 365-page book at the end of one year. Even if I write only half a page, or one page every two days, I will have 182 pages. One letter a week to a loved one, and that's fifty-two times I've shared my love with someone far away.

Gift of Time

By getting up just one hour earlier each morning, I give myself, in one year's time, the gift of at least fifteen extra *full* days. Actually, it's much more than fifteen days, because each of the hours has been well spent. They are prime hours without interruptions.

Risking Failure to Succeed

It is fear of failure that many times keeps us unsuccessful or satisfied with mediocrity. When I recognized that mistakes and failure were my best teachers, I made a big breakthrough. This knowledge offered me a great deal of freedom. Whenever I see myself making a mistake or when someone points one out to me, I quickly ask myself, "What can I learn from this?" By not getting upset and defensive, I allow myself to learn and grow, thereby changing a negative experience into a positive one. I feel that each mistake I make, taken in proper perspective, reduces my chances of making that same mistake again.

We're Not All Alike

Since morning is not the time when I am at my peak efficiency, I have changed my schedule around so that I do my major cleaning and fussing around the house in the evening before bed. I spend a good deal of my morning and early afternoon training and working with my children at their peak time. By becoming aware of my own rhythm, I am no longer forcing myself in the morning, but I am doing my most important work: guiding my children.

There Is Always Tomorrow

It helps to realize that one discouraging day can't decide my future.

Quitting Means I Lose

Whenever I feel I have to struggle beyond my own ability to overcome hardship, I remember that quitting would mean I have lost. Staying with it to the finish adds fiber and strength to my abilities. In finishing anything, from a current crisis to a started project, I acquire stamina for meeting the next challenge and reap the sense of self-gratification that comes with success.

I Don't Have It So Bad

We live close to a large kennel where dogs for the blind are bred and trained. One day when I felt my problems were just too heavy to bear, I had to stop and wait for a frail old man, using his white cane, to get from one side of the street to the other. That evening, upon returning home, I learned that some dear friends had just lost everything in a fire. Some days, like this, are given to teach us gratitude. They help to keep our own problems in perspective.

What Do You Mean, I Won't?

"I can't" really means "I won't." Remembering this helps me see my self-destructive tendencies and gives me deeper insight into the meaning of my own free agency. For instance, if I think I can't do something, like, "I can't get through to Elizabeth," or "I just can't get out of bed earlier," I have limited myself, and I have also blamed my limitation on a lack in myself or on some outside control. However, if I say "I won't," my whole perspective changes. I may still *choose* not to do the thing, but this exercise forces me to see that it is my choice. I apply this principle to all areas of my life, and it is quite therapeutic in producing an inner change.

The Yo-Yo Syndrome

I have been an "up and downer" for years. I pay the price to become organized—then I'm back down into a slump again. I now try to catch myself at the point of going down, when I used to say, "I think I'm going to blow it." Now I say instead, "I'm getting better each time I do this. I will never let myself go all the way down again. Each time I'm down, I come back up a little faster. I may not be perfect yet, but it's getting easier, and the time between ups and downs is getting shorter and shorter." It helps!

Discuss It with Bishop

Once I was torn apart inside because of a particular problem. I mustered up all the courage I could to discuss it with the bishop. I went through every excuse in the world to prevent myself from going, but I finally approached him and poured out my heart. I don't remember any particular advice, but I do remember the feeling of having my worries lifted from my shoulders. When I left the office, I felt comforted and relieved of my burden. He really was a source of strength.

"I Give unto Men Weakness . . ."

The load of feeling guilty and inadequate was lifted from my shoulders when I read this scripture: "And if men come unto me I will show unto them their weakness. I give unto men weakness that they may be humble; and my grace is sufficient for all men that humble themselves before me; for if they humble themselves before me, and have faith in me, then will I make weak things become strong unto them." (Ether 12:27.) The discovery that the Lord gave me those weaknesses to humble me enough to rely on him for strength was enough to make me do just that. I now work on one weakness at a time, relying on His help through prayer and on my own efforts. If the guilt or inadequacy starts to enter my head, I will rid myself of it by remembering the Lord's promise in this scripture.

Just Ask

For some reason, when I need the Lord the most, I find it the most difficult to converse with Him. I have to remember that it's my responsibility to ask for help. He's just waiting to be asked: "And whatsoever ye shall ask the Father in my name, which is right, believing that ye shall receive, behold it shall be given unto you." (3 Nephi 18:20.) What a potent promise! If I could keep it in my heart, then it should be easy to pray.

Develop My Talents

One day a friend asked, "What would you do if you had one entire day to do anything you'd like?" I answered, "I'd want to spend the entire day oil painting. I intend to do it after the children are raised." She replied, "Do you have to wait that long?" I then began to contemplate the possibility of arranging time during the days for practicing my talent. As I discovered ways of accomplishing this without putting my family aside, I became lighthearted and more thrilled with life. I still serve my family and feel they're learning to respect my talent and my quiet time, as well as to bask in the sunshine of my happiness.

"No" to Loneliness

I've suffered from loneliness enough that I don't want to experience it anymore. I decided to do something about it. I will observe someone who looks lonely and then serve that person in the best way I can. I'll spend the evening asking questions about the person, perhaps offer to drive her where she wants to go, or I will invite her to join me in an activity.

Drinking Poison

Holding a grudge against another is like pouring poison into my system. It leads to bitterness and hatred, and causes me to wither inside. I try to rid myself of bad feelings toward others by recognizing them for what they are—my responsibility—and then confessing my weakness, first to the Lord, then to the victims. Usually a misunderstanding has occurred, and we come to peace with each other. However, in some cases, the other person wishes to hang onto the grudge. Then I have to realize that I can't control any one else's actions or feelings; they are that person's responsibility. If I have taken the correct steps for myself, I need not carry any more guilt or bad feelings.

Whittling Away

Sometimes when I have a dreadful task that needs digging into and I just don't feel up to it, I will set the timer for just ten or fifteen minutes. I feel I can endure almost anything for ten minutes. The most amazing thing usually happens: once I've begun the project, I have the desire to continue. If I don't feel like finishing, at least I have begun, and starting again tomorrow will be easier.

Self-Examination

When I'm not feeling a sense of joy, I know something is not right in my life. I examine myself to see what needs to be corrected. When I determine what it is, I get help by observing how others are handling the same problem, by talking it out, or by finding answers through prayer.

The Supermom

Upon introspection, I discovered the most dominant cause of my depressions. It was the feeling that I had to be Supermom, a mother who kept her house spotless, who never yelled at her children, and who greeted her husband at the door with a sweet smile, filled with the desire and energy to serve him in all he requested. Another demand I placed upon myself was that of being the compassionate ward sister who delivered homemade bread or jam to those in need, never failing to say the correct words at the correct times. Of course, I had to be the type of mother whose obedient children would follow after her, spreading happiness and sunshine. These expectations placed pressure, fear, and anxiety upon me that, needless to say, worked against my becoming that woman. When I observed other women achieving in these areas, my feelings of inadequacy only increased. I lost hope. I sank into depression.

What brought me out of it? These simple words to Joseph Smith touch me so forcefully that I contemplated them for days, and then I gradually came to comprehend the Lord's plan: "Do not run faster or labor more than you have strength." (D&C 10:4.)

Walk before Running

I was trying to do more than I could, in reality, do at this time in my life. I was accepting others' expectations as my own. Then I began thinking that there are no expectations placed upon a four-month-old baby to walk. If there were, they would cause him to be nervous and anxious, emotions that would block his attempts and thwart his efforts. I had to face the fact that as a wife and mother, I was like that baby. I couldn't expect to dance the intricate steps of ballet before I learned how to walk. I had never had this experience of being a mother before, so why should I expect more than I was capable of producing? Heavenly Father's plan is to teach me by experience, step by step, precept upon precept. He doesn't expect anything more than my commitment to Him to *try*, proven by effort. I can place my hand in His and let Him take me where He wants me to go—at my speed, not someone else's. I realize that I have a long road ahead of me, but I am at peace knowing it is the plan.

Selected Neglect

I live in an area where there are many strong Latter-day Saint women. They accomplish much and appear to be "perfect," but when I look closely into their lives, I see that they have to give many things up in order to do those things that they do well. Life is filled with discriminating selections between that which we will do and that which we will neglect. It is a fallacy to think that one person can be everything in all facets of her life.

Learning to Like Me

Because I know that one of Satan's greatest weapons is my own negative self-image, I refuse to accept it as a barrier to growth. In the past, I would accept only the good and reject the bad in myself. When I would see stark imperfection, I would fail to see myself as good, lovable, and capable of achieving my real desires. Now I am seeing myself more clearly. I see the real me as the person I am becoming. I am placing more and more trust in my inward desire for perfection. I find that when I am charitable with myself, I change more rapidly than when I hit myself over the head. I am beginning to really like myself for the first time in my life.

One at a Time

I'm working on improving one weakness at a time. I find that if I choose one a month, I'm not overwhelmed. Next month, I'll choose another. I feel good about myself when I overcome each weakness.

Pick and Choose

Whenever I feel boxed in by a problem, I force myself to write down at least three possible solutions. I ask myself, "What can I do right now to improve my situation?" I brainstorm and then pick an alternative solution. By doing this, I'm compelled to see that I could choose another way of solving the problem. Many times I'm amazed at how many possibilities there really are.

Patriarchal Blessing

Whenever I sink into self-doubt, I read my patriarchal blessing. It reassures me of my strengths and warns me of my weaknesses. I then feel the love and understanding of a wise, dear friend, my Heavenly Father.

No Empathy

Many times, when I reach out to others for empathy, they fail to help me. Recognizing the patterns of negative responses has helped me to objectively evaluate my emptiness after seeking their help:

1. Busy Bee: "I'm busy now. Don't bother me."
2. Scientist: "List the facts and leave your emotions out of it."

3. Pollyanna: "Why, there's nothing wrong with you. You're perfect."

4. Fortuneteller: "Everything will be all right."

5. News Columnist: "As soon as you confide in me, I'll get on the phone."

6. Mother: "If you do this and this, then it will be all right."

7. Me-too-Magnifier: "I had that problem too, only worse."

Self-Mastery

I have heard it said that being spiritual is having a mastery over oneself. How do I get that self-mastery? By studying the One who achieved it. I decided to engage myself in a "get-to-know-the-Savior" campaign. I started reading the Doctrine and Covenants and now I'm studying the Book of Mormon. I can see that the first step to self-mastery is to realize that, with the Lord's help, I *can* achieve it.

Where Art Thou?

Even Joseph Smith felt despair and discouragement. He asked "O God, where art thou? . . . How long shall thy hand be stayed?" (D&C 121:1-2.)

I want my children to know that these feelings came even to the Prophet, and that they will get these feelings many times in their own lives. It's what they do with them that counts. What did the Prophet do? He took these feelings to the Lord and waited for an answer. The answer came: "My son, peace be unto thy soul; thine adversity and thine afflictions shall be but a small moment; and then, if thou endure it well, God shall exalt thee on high; thou shalt triumph over all thy foes." (D&C 121:7-8.)

I point out to my children that Heavenly Father was right there. He knew of the suffering and was ready to express comfort and love. It is the same with us. He never deserts us. There is widsom in His allowing us to suffer.

Putting Life on "Hold"

Have you ever found yourself literally pushing a mental button and putting your life on "hold"? I used to do it constantly with such comments as, "When we have enough money, then I'll be happy," "When the children are older, I'll begin reading again," "When I lose ten pounds, I'll feel good once more," or, more commonly, "If I can just get through this crisis, I'll have time for the things that really matter." I had failed to learn that this *is* life, and I am not separate from its problems. It's the process of problem-solving, the making the most of this moment, that matters. In giving up the idea that getting up over the latest trial is the answer, I was able to start enjoying each moment and making every day count.

One Step Back, Two Steps Forward

I have been seriously improving my self-image and self-confidence for the last few years. In watching myself I've found that momentarily failing and stepping backward for a time is really part of my progress and very normal. This knowledge has a steadying effect on me. I try to keep the image of myself as "becoming" or "evolving," in an upward spiral, constantly in my mind. When I'm able to do this, I grow more rapidly. It's the learning and knowledge that we glean from each experience, whether good or bad, and refusing to become discouraged, that keep the growth consistent.

Tell the Truth about Myself

I have a small notebook in which I make lists that tell the truth about myself. I find that without this exercise, I never quite focus into the depth of who I am. With it, I'm able to see exactly what I want and what I feel. Barriers break down, allowing me to achieve goals that previously seemed unobtainable. Examples of topics are:

—Things that I want people to understand about me
—Things I want to stop but am still doing
—Things I want to accomplish
—Something that keeps recurring and won't stop
—Things started and not completed
—Things I want to have but don't have
—Qualities I want to have
—Qualities I want my husband/wife to have
—Things my perfect home will have
—Those to whom I need to apologize
—Talents I want to develop

Clean Out the Ghettos

The ghettos of my closets and cupboards are the ghettos of my mind. If I feel that I'm not progressing, I will clean out something in my environment. It is important to throw items away that are no longer a part of me. When I let go of them, I make room for something new to come into my life.

Letters to Heavenly Father

I can pour out my heart to my Heavenly Father in written form just as I would write to an earthly father. I'm as honest and frank and open with Him as I can be. After I pour out the garbage in the beginning, I then receive comfort, changing the mood of the letters into one of peace, expression of gratitude, and love. Now I have a collection of them that I consider to be a journal of my spiritual growth.

SHARE YOUR SUCCESSES

Dear Reader:

It has been exciting and very gratifying to see the response of our readers to *The Family Idea Book*. Your own ideas and successes have been responsible for the publication of *Family Idea Book II*. We anticipate devoting a future volume to ideas for and about dealing with teenagers. We hope you will once again share your knowledge and experience with us that mothers everywhere may benefit.

Please sent your ideas to:

The Family Idea Book
Editorial Department
Deseret Book Company
P.O. Box 30178
Salt Lake City, Utah 84130

INDEX